"Paul Bennett's memoirs are a rare gem not only for his perspective on his career and work, but for his experiences of a lifetime of travel. Bennett has an excellent style and sense of detail, with wonderful descriptions of the characters he met, of architecture, landscape, cafes, cuisine, and growing up in Toronto. There is professionalism in this work including detailed research into his grandfather's role and death in the First World War and the superb description of Saigon in 1983. To understand how the world actually works one needs accounts like Bennett's descriptions of dealing with Cambodian refugees on the Thai border, organizing the first free election in Cambodia, or helping with the aftermath of the disastrous Asian tsunami of 2004. Altogether, a very enjoyable and valuable read."

--Dr. Ed Whitcomb retired political and economic foreign policy analyst and author
Rivals for Power: Ottawa and the Provinces, the contentious history of the Canadian federation
and *Understanding First Nations: The Legacy of Canadian Colonialism*

"It is rare to find new firsthand accounts from officials who worked on the front lines of Canada's resettlement program for refugees from Vietnam, Laos and Cambodia. Bennett describes with impressive economy and precision how the repression, retribution, and in the case of Cambodia, deliberate genocide, sent millions fleeing by sea and land for their lives. He recounts with compassion how battered survivors did their best to prepare for the interviews that would determine their futures. Bennett portrays with clarity hot, sweaty days of interviewing and the camaraderie that enfolded the national and international officials who did what they could for the refugees. This is an article that would not be out of place on the pages of the *Economist* or the *New Yorker*. Highly recommended."

--Mike Molloy, co-author of *Running on Empty: Canada and the Indochinese Refugees 1975-1980*
and retired Canadian Ambassador and Senior Coordinator of Indochinese Task Force 1979-1980

ON THE BORDER

TWENTY LIFE STORIES FROM FOUR CONTINENTS

PAUL BENNETT

ILLUSTRATIONS: ANOUK'CHET SUONG

 FriesenPress

One Printers Way
Altona, MB R0G 0B0
Canada

www.friesenpress.com

Illustrator: Anouk'Chet Suong

ISBN
978-1-03-911405-0 (Hardcover)
978-1-03-911404-3 (Paperback)
978-1-03-911406-7 (eBook)

1. BIOGRAPHY & AUTOBIOGRAPHY, PERSONAL MEMOIRS

Distributed to the trade by The Ingram Book Company

TABLE OF CONTENTS

PREFACE

Writing a book is something I had not contemplated, although I have to admit that I had tried unsuccessfully to write the occasional short story. But somehow here it is.

There were various reasons for undertaking this project. The first is that I enrolled in an introduction to memoir writing course at Ottawa's Carleton University during the autumn of 2020. This inspired me to write a number of "life stories" (a term I prefer to "memoirs") and not long after that I was surprised to have twenty. Some of the these emanated from the instructor's writing prompts (such as "old photographs" and "cafeterias") and served to provide a wider range of subjects (from the mundane to the extraordinary) than might otherwise have been the case. A description of a family picnic or childhood street is potentially no less interesting than a tsunami. It is all in the telling.

A second reason for writing is that, as I looked back on my life, I was conscious of having witnessed some remarkably interesting Canadian and international events. These include Canada's October Crisis and the influx of Indochinese refugees to Thailand after the Communist takeovers in Cambodia, Vietnam, and Laos. I have also been fortunate to visit some fascinating countries such as Ethiopia during the Communist Derg regime and North Korea only a few years ago. On another occasion, I was lucky to have just avoided a cataclysmic event, the 2004 Indian Ocean tsunami. These experiences are all reflected in this collection.

My stints as a Canadian diplomat and humanitarian program officer with what was then known as the Canadian International Development Agency (now part of Global Affairs Canada) afforded me many international travel opportunities. I also had my parents to thank for instilling in me a sense of adventure and wanderlust at a young age. While I have already been to seventy countries, I suspect that I will be doing less travelling to exotic locales in the future. This is due to the likely long-term travel restrictions and inconveniences brought about by the current COVID-19 pandemic. In addition, in view of the negative effects of increasing international travel upon our climate, there are some places I do not want to leave my human footprint, such as Antarctica.

At the same time, as I reflect on things closer to home, I have noted in some life stories how much social change has occurred over the years. I wanted to document some of this. This includes not only the things one observes as one moves from childhood (as in "The Boy in the Picture") to adolescence ("Kitty's Kitchen") but also how attitudes have evolved in other cases, as I suggest in "Just Slightly Ahead of Her Time."

Having been retired for seven years now, I have been able to spend a considerable amount of time undertaking genealogical research and writing on both sides of my nuclear family. These efforts have led me to want to write more detailed accounts of specific people and events. These are included in "Peter Plays Golf" and "Not More War Stories."

There is another reason for this collection. The creative process has been great fun, as frustrating and time-consuming as it can sometimes be. As someone who studied a considerable amount of history as an undergraduate, the detective work involving Ancestry.ca, Wikipedia, written documents, interviews, and other sources in researching such life stories as "Grandpa Gordon's Grave" has been both rewarding and fascinating.

In most families there is at least one good storyteller. In the case of the Bennett family, it was my father, Peter, although my late sister, Andrea, sometimes lamented the fact that he occasionally forgot a joke's punchline. These stories became part of family lore and were often told at family gatherings and various dinner parties with close friends. As my generation has reached the later stages of life, there is a risk that some of this oral history will be lost forever unless recounted now. Given that various family members have commented that I have an excellent memory, it made some sense for me to undertake this project.

A final reason for putting "pen to paper" or "fingers to word processor" is that the current COVID-19 restrictions have meant that I have been unable to undertake my usual international travel and volunteer work. This has left me with considerable time to do the necessary research, writing, and revision for such a collection. So, if there is any silver lining for me to the current tragic situation, this might be it.

We all have stories to tell. I hope that you will find mine of interest.

PROGENITORS' PICNIC

I am looking at what at first glance is merely a small, faded colour photograph of two somewhat ordinary and sombre seniors in an unidentified location. It is, in fact, an image of my paternal grandparents from 1960. While it reveals many things about them, it leaves others less clear. This is largely because I can recall meeting my grandparents only three times—twice in Canada as a young boy and once in Scotland (and that only for half an hour) as an adolescent. I never had the opportunity to speak to them as an adult. My knowledge of them comes primarily from my father's reminiscences, from which I can no longer benefit due to his death in 1999. The photograph came into my possession accidentally as my siblings and I sorted through my mother's possessions after her death in 2005. Otherwise, it would have been lost forever and would not have prompted me to write this life story.

My paternal grandfather, Theodore Bennett, on the right, was born in Dublin, Ireland, in 1876, to English parents. Grandpa was a banker until he retired in 1928. His wife, my grandmother, Mary Catherine Hally, was born in Glasgow, Scotland, in 1882, into a well-known and successful woolen manufacturing family. After their marriage in 1913, Granny and Grandpa lived primarily in the Greater London Area until retirement, at which time they resided in various English and Scottish towns and villages, finally settling in Kelso in the Scottish Borders.

In this photo, Grandpa has a round, bald head with patches of grey hair above his large ears. I inherited those ears, which became a source of a little teasing while I was in Grade 8 in Ottawa. If Grandpa wore glasses, it is not evident in this or any other photo I have of him. He has a grey casual wool suit with a tie, vest, trousers to just below the knee, and long woolen socks. Grandpa is wearing sturdy brown lace-up shoes, which would have been good for the hillwalking of which he was very fond. Although I can see a wristwatch, he also has a gold chain hanging from his vest, probably to keep his wallet accessible and safe.

Granny is considerably shorter and slenderer than Grandpa, with her long, curly greying hair pulled severely behind her ears. She is wearing a sensible brown jacket with a pink blouse buttoned to the top underneath. Granny appears to be wearing a dark skirt with light-coloured tights and sturdy dark shoes.

Why is neither of them smiling? Were they squinting at the sun or feeling tired from the meal they just ate? Did the photographer (presumably my father) time the photo badly? Or were they from an era and background where emotion was not to be visibly demonstrated? Britons had a reputation for that.

Granny and Grandpa are sitting against a rocky outcrop in some Scottish hills, the exact location of which I am uncertain since there are no identifying features. There is not a tree to be seen in the vast and desolate landscape behind them, a sad result of human deforestation, climate change, wars, and pesky animals. It was no small wonder, perhaps, that one of my Scottish maternal uncles and a cousin became foresters. But I digress. Behind Granny, I see a plain-looking grey sedan of some sort, one of the few ways to get around those remote parts at that time—the other likely being a rural bus network. I don't know if either of them ever learned to drive or owned a car. They certainly would not have needed one when living in London. My father might have driven the day of the picnic.

Grandpa has a white cup of what I assume is tea (or perhaps something stronger) in his right hand. Few Scots drank coffee in those days. That which was available was prepared in a manner which was an embarrassment to the noble crop. British Rail was notorious for its bad coffee, as I could attest in later years during my own travels. Granny and Grandpa's enjoyment of a picnic was something my father and all his children inherited. I can recall cross-country skiing as an adolescent in Gatineau Park near Ottawa with my parents, having to break trail for my parents while carrying a heavy rucksack full of our lunches. These would include sandwiches, cheese with unleavened matzo crackers, fruit, either shortbread or orange digestive biscuits, a bottle of Toby beer, and a big thermos of Bovril with sherry. I'm exhausted just thinking about it. The return trip to the car after these outings with an empty rucksack was always much easier. My father's reputation for culinary treats while in the relative wilds was legendary among my Scottish maternal cousins.

The few trips that Granny and Grandpa took to Canada to visit our family were usually made by Cunard Line cruise ships, considered very romantic perhaps now but the norm in those days. I have seen some of their records of landing in Montreal as part of the genealogical research I have been doing. It is amazing what's available now. About the only thing I recall about their visits as a young boy, however, was playing snakes and ladders when they visited Toronto in the mid-60s. I was a little too young for chess and was envious when my brother, Peter, who was learning the game, challenged Grandpa to a match. My half hour with them as an adolescent at their Kelso seniors' residence in 1970 was not enough to enhance the familial bond.

Three things about Granny and Grandpa have always fascinated me. First, they had the remarkable luck to retire comfortably in 1928, just before the deleterious and long-lasting social and economic effects of the dreadful Depression. Fortunately, they were spared any hardship. Secondly, they lived far longer in retirement than during Grandpa's working years, which would be the envy of many Generation Xers and millennials today. Indeed, a comfortable retirement with pension seems to be the exception rather than the norm now, particularly with the advent of the gig economy and the loss of secure employment due to COVID. Finally, Granny and Grandpa owned a house for only a short period, choosing to live instead in hotels as part of their peripatetic lifestyle. Indeed, they never really learned how to keep house. This is something the casual observer might find odd but was apparently more common in those days.

Since I have been retired for several years now, I have the time to indulge in various interests including embarking on a serious effort to better know and understand my forbears. It's funny how this small and faded cropped picture, which we almost lost track of, fills me with a strange combination of curiosity, regret, and memories.

GRANDPA GORDON'S GRAVE

Our large, modern tour bus pulled up slowly to Euston Road Cemetery outside the village of Colincamps in the Somme, northeast France, on a warm and sunny afternoon. I do not usually travel on organized group tours, but this was part of an ambitious journey in the spring of 2017 to every Canadian and Newfoundland World War I (1914–18) and World War II (1939–45) battlefield and cemetery in France, Belgium, and the Netherlands. While Euston Road Cemetery was not on the normal itinerary, our tour director and guide usually tried to include a visit, where possible, to all those sites of particular relevance to tour participants. We were all appreciative of this opportunity.

I had intended to undertake such a pilgrimage for several years and had felt somewhat guilty at never having visited my grandfather Gordon's grave. All of my siblings, on the other hand, had done so at least once. Finally, the stars aligned. I had been retired since 2014 so had plenty of time. Secondly, I had attended the annual Remembrance Day ceremony in Ottawa and elsewhere for years and was aware of how many of those who had fought to defend our liberty and way of life were dying of old age. A visit to my grandfather's isolated gravesite was a trifling inconvenience compared to his sacrifice. Thirdly, I was conscious of the significant anniversaries of many battles important to Canada, including Vimy Ridge in 1917. Finally, as our tour company had been successfully undertaking such comprehensive excursions for several years, I felt it would have been foolhardy to try to piece together one on my own.

The cemetery was immaculately maintained by the conscientious Commonwealth War Graves Commission. Inside this relatively small property were 1,293 World War I graves. The manicured grass was rich green while the site was surrounded by an attractive three-to-four-foot red brick wall. All the headstones looked remarkably similar from a distance, but upon closer inspection I could not help being struck by the inscriptions. Most of these soldiers who had given their lives were not yet twenty-one, struck down in their prime. Many had barely left school or left shattered sweethearts back home.

Although the cemetery included casualties from various battles in the area, I had come to see my grandfather, Major Reginald Glegg Gordon, who died on March 26, 1918, at the age of thirty-nine. Reginald was born in Valparaiso, Chile, in 1878, where his father had a bookselling and stationary business. Reginald's family returned to

Scotland when he was young so that he could get a Scottish education. After graduating from Edinburgh Academy, Reginald studied medicine at the University of Edinburgh (where he was also a volunteer in the Officer Training Corps of the University Battery of the 1st City of Edinburgh) and the Royal Infirmary. Although he trained as a surgeon, Reginald was subsequently attached to a Scottish psychiatric hospital. He also travelled to Italy to learn more about the new and progressive educational theories of another physician, Maria Montessori. She would gain a significant international reputation with schools based upon her philosophy around the world.

It was not long before Reginald gave up his predictable and reputable career as a medical doctor with the intent of pursuing his first passion, sheep farming. Unfortunately, he could not just become a farmer. He had to apprentice, which meant little or no remuneration before he leased his own land a year later and embarked upon this very speculative profession in earnest. This new life would have created considerable financial hardship for his wife, Barbara, particularly as their young family expanded. Perhaps he had hoped to access his anticipated Chilean inheritance after the death of his father in 1905 to tide himself over to better times. Unfortunately, it was many more years before the estate was settled, well after Reginald's death. The fact that they moved to a remote area in the Grampian Mountains was perhaps not as bad as it might seem, however, as Barbara herself was from a family accustomed to living in distant Scottish places. She was also a nurse (which is how she met Reginald), so probably had a practical side enabling her to cope with such conditions.

Reginald continued, however, with the University Battery and then the Royal Highlanders (Black Watch), eventually attaining the rank of major. When World War I was declared in 1914, he enlisted as a soldier rather than as a medic, somewhat unusual, and spent almost the entire war serving in various capacities in Scotland and France. What must he have thought about leaving his wife and young children when he went to the front? What would happen to his family should he not return? Could he provide for them after his death? What were his hopes for his four daughters? Did he serve solely out of duty to family and country or did he also look forward to joining his comrades at war? Did he fear war's horrors and an agonizing death? From my grandmother's perspective, what did she feel each time he left? Did she have any influence on his decision to go to the front? These are questions to which no answers are fully. Reginald's correspondence to Barbara consisted of little more than postcards addressed in her name but no text!

On March 26, 1918, at age thirty-nine, Reginald was returning from the Battle of Cambrai. This was a major British offensive that marked the first large-scale, effective use of tanks in warfare, a development that would have been frightening and traumatic for all those in the field of battle, including Reginald. Unfortunately, he fell asleep due to extreme battle fatigue and dropped from his horse to the ground. He was immediately crushed by the wheels of a large gun, an extremely ignoble end to the life of someone who had served his family and country well. Indeed, Reginald's efforts over the course of the war had earned him a Mention in Dispatches, where his name appeared

Figure 1

Grandfather Gordon's grave at Euston Road Cemetery in the Somme.

Canton Perdu in the French Pyrenées, where I spent a summer at the age of fourteen.

in an official report describing his gallant action, written by his superior officer and sent to the high command. He was also awarded a Distinguished Service Overseas order (a military decoration of the United Kingdom awarded for meritorious or distinguished service by officers of the armed forces during wartime) prior to his death. His commanding officer noted that "he carried out his duties in an exemplary manner and was a standing example to all others." The battle was also extremely costly for both Britain (and Newfoundland) and Germany, resulting in 75,681 and 54,721 casualties, respectively.

Reginald left his wife (my grandmother) Barbara and four young daughters: Alison (the eldest, at five and a half), Lesley, Barbara, and Jean (my mother), at two and a half years old. His death had a lasting impact on his family. My grandmother never recovered. In some of my mother's life reminiscences, she lamented the fact that she had not known her father. Upon Reginald's death, my grandmother decided to move from their distant farm, Lettoch (which means "plot of land" in Gaelic) to St. Andrews on the east coast of Scotland. There, she was able to enroll her children in a good girls' school, St. Leonards. School authorities had agreed to reduce their fees consistent with an informal policy governing war widows' children at many schools.

Living on a widow's pension at a time when middle-class women were not expected to enter the workforce and would not find appropriate work if they did, had been made more difficult by the fact that much of Reginald's family money was tied up in Valparaiso, as I mentioned earlier. So, although Mum's family grew up having to "watch their pennies" closely, they did have two servants until Mum's marriage in 1940. While we might consider this unusual today, it was common for families of reasonable means at the time. In addition, Grandmother Gordon had a dressmaker come to the house to make clothes for everyone; again, this was not rare then but something that would be considered a luxury today.

There were two incidents during my adolescence that led me to better appreciate the impact of the two World Wars on my mother. The first was on Remembrance Day in 1969. We were watching the ceremony on our old black-and-white television on Birch Avenue in Ottawa. Consciousness regarding Remembrance Day was at a low ebb in Canada, particularly in light of the progressive '60s and the anti-Vietnam War movement. I was finding the proceedings somewhat boring and foolishly suggested that the World Wars were not that relevant to us as nobody in our family had served in the army. I had not really known the circumstances of my grandfather's death. My father immediately took issue and explained the enormous impact of my mother's loss in 1918. The second was in 1970, a few months after the release of the film *Battle of Britain*, which I went to see with my mother. The film included moving images of the horrific bombing of London during World War II. I could see my mother fighting to hold back tears on several occasions. The memories must have come flooding back to her—the loss of her father in World War I, the initial challenges of married life with my father in London during World War II, and the traumatic impact the war had on the emotional health of my Aunt Lesley, who spent much of the war helping children flee the bombing in London.

Many of these thoughts came back to me as I knelt by Grandpa Gordon's grave and then boarded the tour bus after our brief stop. I determined to learn more about his life and wartime experiences, which I have done. I strongly encourage Canadians to visit the war graves in western Europe to pay homage to those who gave their lives so far from home.

PETER PLAYS GOLF

My father, Peter, had many different interests, including mountaineering, travel, fine food and wine, history, and the performing arts. He also enjoyed reading the then multilingual Marmite box while having lunch on Sunday afternoons, which used to amuse family members to no end. But family and close friends would always know him for his love of GOLF!

I can't say exactly when my father swung a golf club for the first time. I suspect he developed his interest from his own father, Theodore, who himself played golf until his mid-eighties. I do know that Peter excelled at the sport while a student at Bradfield College, an independent and (now) co-educational private (although the English would refer to it as "public") school in West Berkshire, England. The college is known for its golf program and facilities including its own nine-hole course. It also, by the way, is the site of a Greek amphitheatre where Peter was proud to have played the lead role in his graduating year thespian production. More to the point, however, he was touched when Bradfield established an inter-school golf medal in his name seventy years later. Peter was chuffed to have been able to attend the commemorative event.

While in his prime and an undergraduate at Hertford College at Oxford University in the early 1930s, he had a handicap of four, no mean feat among competitive amateurs. By this measure he could have called himself a "scratch" golfer, although I never heard him use that term. A few years later, he married my mother, Jean Gordon, a native of St. Andrews, Scotland. In a funny quirk of the day, this entitled him to a membership in what is the home of golf, the Royal and Ancient Golf Club (the R&A), which he assumed with alacrity. Indeed, some family members have playfully suggested that the promise of a membership was the reason he asked for Mum's hand from her widowed mother, Barbara Gordon.

My father remained a member of the R&A for over fifty years, the fact of which he was immensely proud. He did not get to play it much, unfortunately, living "on the other side of the pond" in Canada. In recognition of his faithful membership, however, he was granted a locker on the main floor of the members-only clubhouse, which merely meant that he did not have to walk up and down the stairs to get to the main entrance and bar. I thought this was a rather pathetic display of the club's appreciation but was nonetheless happy to join my proud father for a double port to celebrate this milestone while watching players finishing on the eighteenth green back in 1986. As women are not allowed to join the club or darken the bar as guests even today, my mother, sadly, could not join us.

During part of our family life, we lived in Toronto, where my father worked for Canadian Breweries, then owned by Canadian magnate E. P. Taylor. There, he managed to indulge his passion by being the primary company executive responsible for the short-lived Carling World (Golf) Open, played in 1967 at the Toronto Board of Trade Club, where my father was a member. One of my favourite photos of him is Peter with two accomplished South African and American golfers--respectively, Harold Henning and Bobby Nichols.

During Canada's Centennial year, 1967, my parents were presented in an official capacity to the queen and Prince Philip in Kingston, Ontario, during the official opening of Bellevue House, the residence of Canada's first prime minister, Sir John A. Macdonald. By then we had moved to Ottawa as my father had recently been appointed director of National Historic Sites and Parks. Once held in great esteem, Macdonald has endured some tarnish to his reputation due to his government's Indian Residential School program. During a brief chat, the Duke of Edinburgh, Prince Philip (not always known for his diplomacy) deftly commented on my father's R&A tie, which pleased Dad to no end. This vignette was the subject of various dinnertime stories in the coming months.

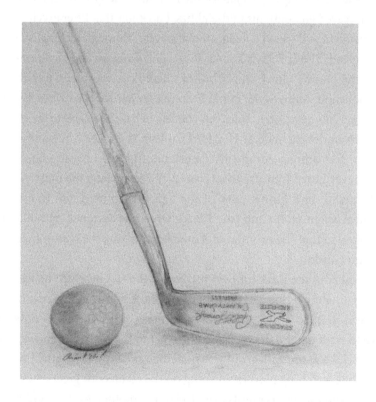

Not long after this, my parents rented a cottage up the Gatineau River from Ottawa in a little hamlet called Kirk's Ferry, about a half-hour drive along the winding Highway 105. My mother and I joined the nearby Larrimac Golf Course and it was not long before my father followed suit. He played and did well in many club tournaments and was pleased to have the occasional match with club member Alison Murdoch, a subsequent four-time Canadian Senior Women's golf champion, as well as the British and Irish Women Senior champion. Dad soon became more actively involved with the club as men's co-captain with his friend Tom Read, and, subsequently, vice president until moving to Victoria, BC, in 1978.

Peter was determined that the youngest boys in his family (Peter Jr. and me) learn how to play the game. I remember he had an old set of his father's wooden golf clubs cut down for me to use. I have kept the putter all these years for purely sentimental reasons as the club is not the easiest to use. I can't say I have ever amounted to much on the links. There is considerable psychology to the game, which my father was able to manage much better than me. I'm not sure whether Dad was disappointed that I did not play better, but if so he never let it show. Watching tournaments on TV and playing with, caddying for, and attending a Canadian (Golf) Open in Montreal are some of my best childhood memories. I still recall some of Dad's expressions while playing. If one of his putts was not long or fast enough, he would mutter, "Paralytic creeper," "Milquetoast," or my favourite, "Gutless wonder," all of which I enjoy using today in his memory.

My parents retired to the Greater Victoria area in 1978, where they were happily able to play year-round due to the mild climate. My father became a member of the prestigious Oak Bay Golf Club, whereas my mother joined another club for various reasons. My parents travelled extensively during their retirement. One trip was to Georgia, USA, to visit an old friend and play the legendary Augusta National course, home of the Masters Tournament, a great thrill for any golfer with a love of the game's traditions.

My nephews Paul and Graham, whom Dad also sought successfully to interest in golf, will no doubt remember the many friendly discussions while washing dishes as to who the best all-time golfer was—Dad's champion, Bobby Jones, or my hero, Jack Nicklaus. This was well before Tiger Woods came onto the scene. As far as I was concerned, there was no contest!

During his last years, Peter suffered from debilitating rheumatoid arthritis, which meant that he had to give up the game, along with hiking, which had succeeded the more rigorous mountaineering as a favoured pursuit. I can remember him rather sadly passing much time in an easy chair reading books on various subjects, including golf. I can't help but think that having to give up the sport had a great impact on his overall enjoyment of life toward the end. But if there is a course in heaven, that is where Peter will be found, rain or shine.

Figure 2

My mother lived on Lettoch Farm in the Grampians before moving to St. Andrews, Scotland.
My father honed his golf skills at Bradfield and Hertford Colleges, England.

JUST SLIGHTLY AHEAD OF HER TIME

It is not possible to look at the course of one's life without considering the roles played by one's parents. My mother's life got off to a somewhat rocky start with the death of her father in World War I. Indeed, she never knew him as he had been serving in the military all of her young life until his death. As traumatic as this event might have been, her mother held the family together as best she could. Mum's studies, at least, did not suffer, as she graduated with an MA in French and German from St. Andrews University. This was no mean feat considering that there were only 9,300 university graduates in the entire United Kingdom in 1938 (which was just after Mum graduated), only 2,240 of whom were women. She then immersed herself in languages, living in Germany and France, something quite unusual for a woman of her day. She began her working life with the British Liberal Party, although not necessarily out of conviction to the Party's beliefs. With the outbreak of World War II in 1939, she went to work in the British Ministry of Information in the Balkan and French sections. Upon my parents' marriage in 1949, however, she was required to give up her employment, as society demanded of women at that time. Exactly a year after their marriage, Mum gave birth to her first child, Barbara, who represented a new phase of their married life. During this first period of her life, my mother demonstrated considerable tenacity and perseverance against significant odds, successfully challenging some gender norms while abiding by others.

Mum and Dad moved to North America in 1943, where Dad first served as the UK Ministry of Information delegate to the United Nations in New York City. In the years that followed, Mum primarily played the part of a loving helpmate to and enabler for her husband and family, a more socially acceptable, gender-specific role. She gave birth to four more children over the next twelve years while also having several miscarriages. Such a large family was common and even desirable in the postwar baby boom. They moved at least twelve times during that period, including to New York City, Ottawa, Oakville, Stratford, West Vancouver, Toronto, and a return to Ottawa. In the case of the latter, they moved houses three times in four years. These frequent changes do not include a short stay in Scotland in 1950 at the time of her mother's death and temporary accommodation in various locations while waiting for more suitable or permanent housing. It would have fallen to Mum to bear most of the burden of these moves, as society expected of her.

From 1946 to 1970, Mum supported Dad as he changed employment five times. In addition to taking a keen interest in what he did professionally and providing the moral support he would have required to make such transitions, she was also an enabler in his work, particularly during the early days of the Stratford Shakespeare Festival (1955–58). As managing director, Dad worked with the likes of Tyrone Guthrie, William Hutt, Lorne Greene, and Christopher Plummer, who all became icons of Canadian and international stage and screen. Mum was right there supporting Dad, entertaining and assisting in ways not always obvious to the casual observer. As an example, Mum and Dad were able to lend our family christening gown to the Plummers, who were in Stratford only temporarily, given the seasonal nature of the theatre, after the birth of their daughter. Mum's dedication to the arts and support of my father was repeated in West Vancouver during Dad's tenure as general manager of the Vancouver International Festival. As a side note, my brother Peter (only six years old at the time) remembers meeting the famous French mime, Marcel Marceau, and was amazed to discover that Marceau could actually talk!

This brings me to our years in Toronto, during which Mum played a further behind-the-scenes role volunteering in the administration and promotion of the Museum Children's Theatre (MCT) and Young People's Theatre with Susan Douglas Rubes, a Canadian TV and screen actor. Her dedication was such that I recall that Mum convinced me to buy a $100 bond to help ensure the financial success of the MCT. Talk about "having skin in the game" at a young age! Mum's community involvement carried over to Ottawa, where we moved in 1967 when Dad became director of National Historic Sites and Parks. There she was active at Christ Church (Anglican) Cathedral where she served as president of the Anglican Church Women, which required her to give much of her time and effort.

By 1970, I was the only child left at home and halfway through secondary school, thus needing much less of Mum's time. As a result, she began to feel a little restless and in search of more challenge in her life. Consequently, she enrolled in the Bachelor of Library Science program at the University of Ottawa at the advanced age of fifty-five. The program was for those who already had a BA and it was normally undertaken over the course of two years. Never resisting a challenge, Mum decided to do it in one. This necessitated a considerable amount of determination and fortitude on her part. She had many late nights writing essays and studying for exams. Mum was lucky to have completed the program when she did as it was terminated a year after her graduation. During her demanding studies, she was wife to a husband who was often travelling for business, mother to an adolescent boy, and an active community volunteer.

Graduation and subsequent employment as a librarian in Canadian acquisitions at the National Library of Canada gave Mum some career satisfaction and a measure of independence. It also provided the opportunity to contribute financially in a significant way to the family for the first time since World War II. The extra income meant that Mum and Dad were able to buy a wonderful cottage up the Gatineau River in Québec outside Ottawa, where we spent many wonderful summers reading, swimming, entertaining, and playing golf.

I was the youngest son and did not go away to boarding school as did my brothers, who both attended Ridley College in St. Catharines, Ontario. I chose instead to stay in a nurturing home environment and attend the public Lisgar Collegiate Institute in Ottawa. It was my mother who provided much of the support a teenager requires during my father's frequent business travel. She was always there in times of need, sometimes helping me cram for tests and nurturing my own interests and opinions. I recall going to John Turner's Liberal nomination meeting in the new riding of Ottawa-Carleton in 1967 as she wanted me to learn more of the political process in Canada. Turner, of course, went on years later to briefly be Canada's prime minister. I took an interest in politics after that and studied politics as an undergraduate. From quite a different perspective, she also taught me the importance of a good night's sleep, that whatever problem a teenager might be wrestling with could always seem more manageable in the morning.

Mum and Dad retired to the rural municipality of Metchosin on Vancouver Island, BC, in 1978. Their home was their dream retirement house, which they had built for them while they were still living in Ottawa, necessitating many long-distance phone calls with the realtor, architect, and builder. This was before the benefit of WhatsApp, where you can see in real time the person you are in conversation with. That Mum and Dad would choose to move across the continent again was a testament to their courage and adaptability, as well as their growing aversion to the cold Ottawa winters! They were also keen to be closer to two adult children (Barbara and David) and their families, although it did mean leaving behind my brother Peter in Toronto and me in Kingston, although I would temporarily move out west for a few years upon graduation from my master's program at Queen's University.

Mum and Dad threw themselves into life in Greater Victoria wholeheartedly, spending time with family while joining two different churches and golf clubs. Her supportive efforts in theatre manifested themselves once again as Dad became president of the Bastion Theatre Board, one of Victoria's two professional thespian companies, now unfortunately no longer in existence. Dad's presidency meant considerable entertaining as well as providing some support to the ensemble. On one occasion, Mum and Dad invited the artistic director and his same-sex partner, who had just moved to the city as a couple, to live in their house while Mum and Dad were on an extended trip to Europe. Their acceptance of this living arrangement was considered progressive during the late 1970s.

I would be remiss if I did not mention the importance of travel beginning early in my mother's life. This was exemplified by her immediate post-graduate months in France and Germany and decision to move to London after that, which I have already mentioned. Upon their arrival in Canada, they made a point of seeing as much of the country as possible and often took us with them. In 1967, five of us (Mum, Dad, Andrea, Peter, and myself) packed up a Ford station wagon and set out to visit every existing and potential national historic site from Ottawa to Vancouver Island with some provincial ones thrown in for good measure. This adventure gave us children a much better appreciation for Canada than we had had to that point. Alas, Mum never got around to finishing the diary she kept on this trip and to which we contributed every morning as Dad drove.

Mum was also able to do some international trips during their Ottawa years (in addition to her regular trips to the UK, partly to see family), accompanying Dad on business to places such as Scandinavia. It was during retirement, however, that Mum's love of travel flourished. They travelled extensively in Australia, Europe, Asia, and North America. One of the highlights was a six-month journey through Western Europe, Thailand (where I was at the Canadian Embassy), India, Nepal, and China. This trip was exotic by any standard and included a three-week trek in Nepal's Annapurna Sanctuary at age seventy. As I grow older, I marvel at this accomplishment.

During these years, Mum was more of an equal to my father but also provided much needed support to him during his later years with rheumatoid arthritis. This she did at the expense of her own health, choosing to focus on his illness, probably shortening or at least diminishing the quality of her life considerably.

It is time to put the finishing touches to this portrait. To paraphrase the old Panasonic advertising slogan, my mother might have been considered "just slightly ahead of her time" in some regards. Yet she was also one who had to live within the confines of contemporary gender roles. Throughout her life, she demonstrated her commitment to family and her adopted country of Canada and community, and her traits of adaptability, resourcefulness, determination, and selflessness. These qualities stood her well over her lifetime and are ones that we, as children, have taken on board with enthusiasm.

NOT MORE WAR STORIES

It is important to know how my parents met. They were both working at the British Ministry of Information (MOI) just prior to the outbreak of World War II. This ministry was created twice—once during each World War for the purposes of wartime publicity and propaganda, censorship, and the monitoring of public opinion. After graduation from St. Andrews University in Scotland, Mum had gone to Hamburg and Munich to improve her German and then to France for more French, naturally. Following her European language immersion, Mum moved south from Scotland to London, where she completed a nine-month business course for women, providing her with practical skills to seek clerical employment. At that time, a woman could not expect to find employment commensurate with her skills and abilities and would always be paid less than a man if she were able to find appropriate and commensurate work

Upon graduation from Hertford College of Oxford University, Dad began his professional career with the film section of the MOI, which collaborated closely with the Foreign Office. On one occasion, Mum and Dad were riding in the same Foreign Office elevator as Sir John Thomas Pratt, a seasoned British diplomat and the brother of William Henry Pratt. The latter was a well-known British actor whose stage name was Boris Karloff, the star of horror films such as *Frankenstein*. According to Dad's reminiscences, Sir John introduced the two of them to each other for the first time. Mum, on the other hand, recalled that they had already met. At any rate, she was somewhat in awe of this man due to his distinguished career, so she began talking to Dad as a diversion. I am not sure which was true, but the rest was history, as the saying goes. Mum and Dad agreed to get together for a date that weekend. For years after, Dad enjoyed telling people that he and Mum had been introduced by Frankenstein's brother, which always elicited many belly laughs. Although being introduced by a monster might not bode well for some relationships, Mum and Dad did well, staying together for almost sixty years, until the time of Dad's death.

Shortly after their engagement, Dad was sent on a tour of the Balkans in Central Europe, including Albania and the former Yugoslavian countries, as well as Turkey, Greece and Egypt. Sadly, Hitler had the uncanny knack of taking over a country just as Dad left it. Upon arriving in Cairo, therefore, toward the end of his voyage, he immediately cabled Mum asking that the wedding date be fixed earlier than planned and that the banns be published in her church immediately. This was a perquisite to getting married in a Church of England wedding.

But their courtship was not always smooth, as can be expected with any couple. On one occasion, they met for tea and pastries on a Sunday afternoon at a London café they both enjoyed. According to Mum, Dad ogled the sweet offerings a little too fondly, focussing more on which pastry to lovingly devour rather than Mum's conversation. So, rather than playing second fiddle to an inanimate chocolate éclair, Mum got up in a huff and charged out of the restaurant without a word. It is not clear whether Dad ran after her, as a devoted fiancé should, or remained at the table to consume his pastry (and possibly my mother's, as well).

Mum and Dad lived in London during the Battle of Britain in 1940 at the beginning of their married life. During this time, the German air force sent up to 160 bombers a night across the English Channel, raining down death and destruction. As a result, Mum and Dad, like most Londoners, regularly took shelter in the Underground ("the Tube"). The situation became so acute, however, that once Mum became pregnant with Barbara, she returned north to St. Andrews, Scotland, for the birth.

Due to shortages of most consumer goods during wartime Britain, Mum and Dad learned to reuse and repurpose everything they had—clothing, furniture, books, food—as did most of their generation, a habit they never really lost, much to the displeasure of some of us siblings in later years. We learned to reuse tin foil, plastic bags, and Christmas wrapping paper religiously. We sometimes asked each other if we would ever get a present of sports equipment or clothing that was not a "hand-me-down." It was certainly ironic that, during the 1970s, when recycling and environmentalism became prominent and popular, Mum and Dad were already ahead of the game.

Mum and Dad, as well as my sister Barbara, boarded the luxurious Cunard Queen Mary ocean liner at Gourock, Scotland, on September 4, 1943, destined for New York, where Dad was to represent the MOI at the United Nations. The Queen Mary had, like other passenger ships, been retrofitted as a troop carrier (known perhaps somewhat ominously as "the Grey Ghost") to aid the Allied war effort, often transporting more than 15,000 soldiers at a time. As a result, it was under constant threat of attack by German U-boats, which would obviously have been very traumatic for those civilians aboard. Barbara was required to wear a lifejacket the entire voyage, which any young child would find difficult. What made things worse for was the fact that the film *The Sinking of the Lusitania* (which was the name of a Cunard Ocean liner sunk by the Germans in 1915) or *The Titanic* (Barbara and I are not sure which) was screened for the passengers' diversion. Either would have undoubtedly frightened the passengers even more than was already the case. Clearly, the person in charge of entertainment had not done their homework or thought of the consequences.

The Bennett family arrived in New York on September 10, 1943, where they would spend three years living in three different houses or apartments, a peripatetic affliction that dogged our family for many years. By the time they moved to Ottawa in 1946, the war was over, and a more normal life could resume, although they would never forget their wartime experiences.

SCHOOL POOL

I am reflecting on first learning to swim with mixed emotions. I attended Allenby Public School on Avenue Road in what was then known as North Toronto from age seven to eleven. As I remember the school, it was an imposing two-storey brick building set back from Avenue Road by a spacious front playground, which included generous track-and-field facilities. But the memory plays tricks on people and perhaps the alma mater is not quite as grand as I recall. Or alternately it has shrunk. On the far side of the building were separate entrances for boys and girls. I am not sure why the genders were segregated. What did school authorities think we would get up to when merely walking through the same door?

I recall other things about the school. In the lower grades, we would often play Danish Rounders during recess, boys and girls together. This game isn't played much anymore but it involved kicking a volleyball outside the inner pitch area and running around the bases. The popcorn man, a recent Italian immigrant, was always waiting for us at street side at recess, lunch time, and after school with his little white-and-silver cart. I was jealous of the other children whose parents would regularly give them five or ten cents for a small bag, which the popcorn man would slather with buttery grease.

There was also the occasion when my brother Peter and I were called inside the school during recess on a particularly cold, late November day. The teachers were concerned for our welfare as we were still wearing our shorts while the other boys had switched to long pants weeks earlier. We were a little embarrassed to have this attention drawn to us. Apparently, our mother thought such sufferance would be character building. Perhaps she was right as we didn't complain about it at the time.

I recall my elation at the end of Grade 3, when I had finally learned how to ride my rather dilapidated red bike and was able to take it to school like the other boys. What independence and confidence that gave me. A few years later, I was given a combination odometer and speedometer for my birthday. In response to a challenge from Peter, I would get up before breakfast just to see how many miles I could put on my new CCM bike, which I purchased from saving my pocket money and meagre pay for singing in the local church choir. I am not sure that many churches can afford choirboy remuneration now.

Although North Toronto was a fairly homogenous WASP neighbourhood at that time, there were a few exceptions. I recall two Middle Eastern brothers whose family had just moved to Canada being absolutely amazed at their first snowfall one cold November. It was a challenge to get them back inside after recess. There was also a Singaporean boy whose father came to a school assembly (an event that was always eagerly anticipated) to talk about his country of origin. About the only thing I remember from his speech was that Colgate and other products were often imitated in Southeast Asia. They were sold with such names as Gatecol in the local markets, which we all found hilarious. Little did I know that I would subsequently live in Southeast Asia and work on such subject files as copyright infringement.

But perhaps my strongest memory (or trauma) was of the swimming pool. The school was lucky to have a large indoor one, where we had classes once a week, beginning in Grade 3. Students from other schools would come to Allenby to learn their strokes, just as we would go to nearby John Ross Robertson for industrial arts, also known a little less glamorously as "shop." And the girls would do home economics.

I don't remember anything about the changing room or shower. Did we have to line up before going in? Did it have blue walls for boys and pink for girls? I guess none of that is particularly important now. But I do recall how much I dreaded the mandatory swim classes. I would stay up the night before worrying about whether I could master the flutter kick, at first, or the front crawl after I had advanced a little. Could I keep up with my more able classmates like Carol Lang and Paul Kent? Even at that young age, Paul worked in the unusual capacity as an undertaker's assistant in the evenings and on weekends. We all went on to the new Glenview Senior Public School together and Carol went on to university, I think. I am not sure what Carol is up to, but Paul is a successful funeral director outside Toronto, having been licenced now for forty-two years. How many of us can say we have spent so long doing something we really enjoy?

The one exception to that late-night fretting was if Foster Hewitt were broadcasting a Leafs game, in which case my brother and I would listen under the covers with our headphones glued to our ears. In those days, we shared a bedroom, as did most siblings of similar ages. Pictures of the royal family complete with corgis adorned our age-appropriate racing car wallpaper. I have to say that the thought of those posters makes me cringe a little now.

My worrying got so bad that my mother called my homeroom teacher, Mrs. Brown, to let her know how I was feeling. So, Mrs. Brown talked to the young swimming instructor (who I am sure we thought was ancient). She pulled me aside during one January class to say that I should only do what I could manage, which just made me worry more. While she was clearly trying to reassure me, I interpreted her offer as a criticism of my swimming skills. And what if the other kids had heard this conversation? They would just make fun of me. Those classes affected my self-confidence back then and it did not help that my brother Peter seemed much more competent in sports than me.

While my swimming career at Allenby was less than stellar, summer camps and Red Cross classes changed all that. I eventually became very proficient and even joined our high school water polo team, although I can't say I saw a lot of pool time in our league games. I now get great satisfaction swimming several days a week, either inside or outdoors, depending on my location and the climate. For me, swimming is both relaxing and a great way to stay in shape.

The school pool is now in the hands of private enterprise and swimming is no longer part of the curriculum, as is the case for school pools around Toronto. According to my niece, a former long-time camp counsellor and recreation director, this has meant that campers today do not have the same pool skills as before, which is unfortunate. I can now look back at those first swimming lessons with some detachment, insight, and amusement, but that hardly benefits the nervous eight-year-old boy of the time.

THE BOY IN THE PICTURE

I have another old photo in front of me. There I am, crouching slightly while standing on a Toronto street playing road hockey, my favourite childhood winter sport, as it was for most Canadian boys of my age. I was never any good at skating but loved the street version. I'm smiling while waiting for the ball to come to me, wearing my green-and-white striped Glenview Senior Public School winter tube hat. I didn't care much for the school but liked the hat well enough. I'm an average height for a twelve-year-old boy. I have one of my favourite jackets on, a reversible black-and-red parka with a blue, handwoven woolen turtleneck sweater underneath, popular at that time. I always looked forward to my older brother David coming home from boarding school so we could play an extended game with the neighbourhood kids. What boy of my age doesn't remember shouting "Car!" picking up the net and moving to the side of the street as a motorist cautiously drove by? It's too bad that street hockey has been banned in so many cities. Where will the next Hockey Night in Canada fans come from?

For some reason there are no parked cars in the background of the picture. Was this because some kind neighbours had moved their vehicles so we could play unimpeded that afternoon? That wouldn't surprise me at all. Many of our neighbours were like that. Edie Frankel, who lived across from us, had an abandoned tennis court with high fences at either end beside her house. We were always welcome to play football or baseball whenever we wanted. How good was that? Her son Blair was just a little too small to play with us big boys. We had some wonderful times there, scoring brilliant goals, smashing home runs, and making outlandish bets on who was going to win the next Argonaut football game. Edie employed a maid by the name of Aida, who always promised to take my brother Peter and me to a Toronto Maple Leafs baseball game. That was way before the Blue Jays came to town. Sadly, we never got to that game before we moved to Ottawa in the summer of 1967. Edie died a few years ago and I am sure that Aida did so long ago. She seemed much older than Edie back then and, as a domestic, had probably lived a harder life so her life expectancy was probably shorter.

Now that I think about it, it's probably a staged photograph I am looking at. There may have been no other people playing beside myself. This was because we were always dutifully posing so my father could send pictures back to our doting grandparents in Scotland. I had only met them twice by then, so this was one of the few forms of contact we had. But Granny and Grandpa ensured we did not forget them. They faithfully sent parcels of Penguin biscuits, licorice all sorts, chocolates, Edinburgh rock, and Turkish delight from Littlejohn and Son Confectioners in Glasgow, to mark everyone's birthdays and important holidays like Christmas and Easter. They knew their way to a child's heart (or stomach, in this case). No wonder we all have a sweet tooth.

Any account of my life as a boy in Toronto would not be complete without reference to our family dog, a wonderful border collie by the name of Polly. She roamed free in those days as dogs were allowed to do except when we got a call from Dr. Klute a few doors down to complain that she had dug up his flowerbed. We could never understand why he was so upset but I am sure our gardening parents did. We sometimes fed her table scraps, which probably wasn't that healthy for her, nor was the fact that she stayed outside for much of the long and sometimes bitter Toronto winters. Her death one late January day was a sad event for us and all the neighbourhood kids who had adopted her over the years.

Up the street from Edie and Blair Frankel lived Billy, whom Peter and I thought was really cool. He was a long-haired American with a buckskin jacket and Davey Crockett hat along with a replica Civil War revolver of some sort, perhaps a derringer. We formed a club of three one summer and made our fort in the back of our garage, using an old mahogany cupboard door to keep the world out. I'm not sure my father thought that was the best use of such fine wood. Non-members could not enter, including David. Billy moved with his family up to the Bridal Path neighbourhood, so we only saw him once or twice after that.

The house to the right of ours belonged to Mr. Cousens and his wife. If they had any children, they had long moved away by the time we moved there in 1962. But I think he still wanted some around, so he took a shine to us. An exceedingly kind man, he worked for Clarke Irwin, a major Canadian-owned publisher in those days, responsible for bringing such rising luminaries as Robertson Davies and Timothy Findley to public attention. He paid my brother Peter and me handsomely for shovelling snow every winter. This was no mean task as the City of Toronto did not plough municipal sidewalks in our neighbourhood so we had to do that as well as their wide and steeply sloped driveway. We bought our first leather football with the proceeds one year. In fact, I pulled it out just the other day. Unfortunately, the old arm is getting a little stiff with arthritis so I won't be stepping onto the gridiron any time soon. But I learned the value of money in those days since I was also a bicycle delivery boy for Brisebois Pharmacy, just off Yonge Street. For that I was paid the princely sum of eighty cents an hour. Alas, I was unlikely to get rich as I worked only two hours a week. Being asked to deliver to Loretto Abbey far to the north was a treat since I would have lots of time to enjoy the scenery and fresh air.

Beside the Cousens' house were Teddy and his parents. His father was English and his mother German. I remember Teddy calling her *Mutti*, a word I learned a few years later when studying German at Glenview. Although Teddy was a few years younger than me, we still enjoyed playing together after school and on weekends. I'm not sure what school he went to but it wasn't ours. One afternoon, Teddy and I went to see a children's movie at the long-since shuttered neighbourhood Capitol Theatre. While walking home I suddenly decided that he was too young to be my friend anymore. I am not sure why I felt that way but we didn't see much of each after that. I sometimes felt a little guilty about that for years after.

Across the street and to the west of Edie Frankel's was "the ravine," part of a wonderful network of undeveloped forest that runs throughout much of Toronto. We would snake our way through there to the Lytton Tennis Club and Glenview School. I remember spending a lot of time in the ravine chasing squirrels, smoking the occasional cigarette, and playing "kick the can" in one of the open areas. Or we'd eat some of the candy we bought from Sandy's Smoke Shop on Yonge Street. One time we were astonished to find a paper bag full of handcuffs and bloody white shirts. My brother Peter recalls feeling very grown up after telling Mum about our discovery, as she then called the police. There were lots of rumours about why these items were there, but we never really found out what the truth was.

We were princes of the streets in those days. Having bikes gave us real independence, at least as far as that goes at age eight or nine. We could walk or bike everywhere, all the while feeling safe. We would ride to the church, where we sang in the choir and attended Sunday school, Wolf Cubs, and summer camps. My parents were unflinching believers in parish church life and the stalwarts who shaped our lives there. Our neighbour Edie's son Blair did not go to church as his family was Jewish, something that was always a bit of a mystery to us.

And did I mention the familiar family bell? My mother had brought a gold-coloured bell in our move from Vancouver that she would ring to summon us for tea or lemonade while we were playing baseball or hockey or building our garage fort. Nobody gave us a hard time about that bell or accused us of being attached to Mum's apron strings, although in retrospect they could have. Mum still had that bell until she had to move into a Victoria seniors' home forty years later where she would not have room for her lifetime of possessions and memories.

Those were formative years. I became a lifelong Maple Leafs fan, which turned out to be tough love since they haven't won the Stanley Cup since 1967, but I live in hope. I went to lots of camps, began to play golf, and learned how to ride a bike. I was of the age where I learned that some of the friendships I formed at school or church were fleeting, just as many of the businesses I have written about closed over they years. All of this occurred within the safe confines of my family, which changed somewhat when we moved to Ottawa in 1967, and I began to spread my adolescent wings.

KITTY'S KITCHEN

It is not my mother's kitchen I am writing about. In fact, we moved house so many times as a family that there is no one single kitchen that comes to mind more than the others. No, I am writing about a kitchen thousands of miles away in the foothills of the French Pyrenees. I was there for a short time when much of the Western world was engaged in tumultuous protest against the Establishment, accepted norms, and American involvement in the Vietnam War. But far from a place of unsettling change, Kitty's kitchen offered much-needed warmth and security for a fourteen-year-old boy far from home and the things he knew.

I was spending the summer of 1970 at the age of 14 with Kitty and Maurice de Bellefeuille in Canton Perdu, Ariege, on an idyllic mountain farm. I was there to learn French and absorb the local culture in exchange for my parents' Canadian dollars (which were then valued at more than US greenbacks) and my meagre contribution of labour. Maurice was originally from France and Kitty from England. They moved to Canada in the mid-1960s and ran a stereo and television business in Elliott Lake, Ontario where the future of uranium mining looked promising. When their enterprise failed, the de Bellefeuilles returned to France, working on farms throughout the country, deciding where they wanted to put down roots. Having chosen Canton Perdu, they lived on a meagre pension and consumed what they grew or raised themselves. Every year they would invite a Canadian boy to join them and I was the third. Previous to me there had been the sons of diplomats-turned-authors and academics, George Ignatieff and Douglas LePan.

Kitty was more than fluent in French at a time when few Brits could claim to be so. She dressed plainly, appropriate to their farming lifestyle, often in baggy blue jeans or pale green shorts in summer. Kitty never worried with make-up, nor with the appearance of her thick, waist-length hair, usually tied loosely with an elastic band. In her few spare moments, she loved painting with oils, still life or breathtaking views of the rolling farms, forests, rivers, and distant chateaux visible from their balcony, all the while listening to classical music.

Maurice was also fluent in English and French. He had been interned during the Second World War and subsequently became a member of the *Résistance*. Maurice took to farming quickly, enjoying the outdoors and the independence a farm gave him, despite the uncertainties of weather, crops, and income. Tanned and handsome, Maurice spent most days wearing no more than tiny red shorts and tattered running shoes. He had a dark side, however. His short stature and the fact that the war prevented him from going to university probably contributed to an inferiority complex, particularly since Kitty was a Cambridge graduate. Maurice's time as a prisoner of war likely also affected his nerves. These factors manifested themselves, at least in part, in occasional and unpredictable fits of rage of which I was fearful during my summer there.

On my first day on the farm, I burned my back and arms severely while digging up weeds in one of the terraced garden plots, unaccustomed to the direct sun at high altitude. Kitty gently administered to my aching body as I wondered how the rest of the summer would go. But I quickly adapted to the daily routine, rising early for breakfast followed by chores like escorting the squawking ducks to their outdoor enclosure, picking fruit, and scything hay for winter fodder. I would occasionally be sent with freshly picked berries as a gift for their closest neighbours, Marie and Sévrain, in Cautirac, a nearby hamlet, to practise my French.

Maurice and Kitty had no telephone, which I grew to appreciate as I loved the solitude. And, of course, I didn't know anyone in the area to chat with anyway. *Le facteur* came only twice per week with letters from family and friends as well as newspapers and magazines. *Le Canard enchaîné* was a satirical review and one of the few pleasures Maurice and Kitty could afford. After the postman left, we would retire to our respective bedrooms or the shade of a tree for a quiet hour of reading. This would be followed by more chores or a relaxing afternoon of mushroom picking on the nearby mountain slopes.

The farmhouse was a ramshackle old set of once-separate homes that they had joined together, much wider than deep. Common wisdom would have suggested that it was in such a poor state that it could never have been home for any family, but somehow, over the years, they had made it theirs. Their kitchen was accessible from the front yard, but to call it a kitchen was a bit of a stretch. Sure, it had a long table with chairs, a stove, shelves, and a fridge, most of the essential elements. But there was no running water so vegetables were washed at the little well down the hill during the warmer months. Dirty dishes had to be carried upstairs through Maurice and Kitty's bedroom, down a long hall stacked with tattered books to the bathroom, where they would be washed after each meal.

I have many fond memories of that kitchen. On one of my first mornings there, Kitty and I laughed together after she discovered that I had mistakenly brought back for breakfast a large, ribbed rubber or plastic egg designed to encourage hens to lay. I remember a wonderful birthday dinner of roast duck and potatoes, French cut green beans, and salad, all freshly harvested, followed by apple crumble. I luxuriated with a small glass of wine (I was only fourteen at the time!) to toast the occasion, proud to have learned a few more words of French that day. We would watch *Les Shadoks* on TV most nights, a wildly popular, non-sensical cartoon. I am not sure I understood anything about it, but I enjoyed being surrounded by those who did and was perhaps a little afraid to show my ignorance.

But most of all, I loved our tea times, more English than French, on Saturday afternoons, just before our last turn in the fields or vegetable patches, followed by Sundays off. Kitty would make a huge pot of Ceylon tea, kept warm by an oversized handknit tea cozy. We would happily snack on freshly baked cookies or raspberry tarts, the contents of which we had picked a few hours earlier. We would exchange stories of our work that week or what we planned to do the next day together. Maurice rarely talked about the war, although he eventually published his memoirs, which went on to garner considerable praise.

I returned to Canada at the end of that summer and entered Grade 11, where I found that my French had improved considerably. I would use some of the phrases and expressions I had picked up that summer to impress my French teacher. I managed to visit again in January 1978, when the mountains were magically blanketed in snow. Unfortunately, Kitty and Maurice divorced a few years after that. They are both now long dead. But my memories remain strong. It was probably partly due to that summer that I developed a sense of travel. I attempted several times to get in touch with one of their sons a few years ago with no luck. But I plan to go back over the next few years in a post-COVID-19 world to what I understand is still a wonderfully unspoiled part of France.

OPERATION GINGER

Few Canadians of a certain age can easily forget the October Crisis of 1970. But for those born after those fateful events, let me provide a little background. During the 1960s and 70s, Québec's radical separatist movement was very active. On October 5, 1970, the Front du libération du Québec (FLQ) kidnapped British trade commissioner James Cross in Montreal in pursuit of its aims. In response to pleas from Québec Premier Robert Bourassa and Montreal Mayor Jean Drapeau, Prime Minister Pierre Elliott Trudeau (Justin's father) deployed the Armed Forces and invoked the *War Measures Act* on October 16, the only time it was applied during peacetime in Canadian history. According to these emergency regulations, the FLQ was outlawed and membership became a criminal act. Three thousand arrests and detentions were authorized without charge as normal civil liberties were suspended. Most were subsequently released without the laying of any charges. On October 17, the body of Pierre Laporte (who had been abducted and killed by the FLQ) was found in the trunk of a car. Laporte had been Québec deputy premier, parliamentary leader, minister of immigration, and minister of labour and manpower (yes, he held all those positions!). Laporte was one of the few politicians to be assassinated in Canada, another being Thomas D'Arcy McGee, a Father of Confederation.

The reaction to the invocation of the *War Measures Act* was mixed. Although most Canadians were initially in favour, many changed their views as it was seen to have been a major attack on civil liberties. I remember discussing this at the time with my good friend Jack Gibbons, who was vehemently opposed. Neither did senior soldiers appreciate this shift of their responsibilities from defence to internal national security. From a federalist perspective, the event galvanized Québec separatists against the use of force to gain Québec sovereignty.

Outside the province of Québec, the impact of these developments was most obvious in the National Capital Region. Our family was living in the village of Rockcliffe Park (now part of Ottawa), the home to cabinet ministers, diplomats, and senior public servants, many of whom required protection during the October Crisis. As part of Operation Ginger, the 3rd Battalion of the Royal Canadian Regiment assisted the Ontario Provincial Police (responsible for policing the village) and the RCMP. Imagine the children's excitement when the army pulled up to Rockcliffe Park Public School one day to set up camp. The younger students, of course, had no idea why this was happening.

In my neighbourhood, a newer development on the far side of MacKay Lake, lived Defence Minister Donald Macdonald, Finance Minister Edgar Benson and the clerk of the Privy Council Gordon Robertson (the most important public servant of the day and political advisor to Prime Minister Trudeau), all requiring special protection. The army had a tank at the ready on Robertson's lawn throughout this period.

About that time, our family adopted a black puppy mutt named Sheenagh (a Gaelic name suggested by my Scottish mother). Sheenagh was curious about everything and greeted all those she met without discrimination, as most puppies do. I would take her on my *Globe and Mail* paper route (in the days when boys would deliver the paper on foot or bike in time for breakfast as opposed to adults driving a longer route in the early hours of the morning, as is the case today). She would zig-zag wherever she pleased, totally oblivious to my commands to heel. My problem was that I had to get through the phalanx of soldiers to the doorstep of each of these prominent Canadians to deliver their newspapers. Upon first seeing me with Sheenagh, the soldiers smirked and let us through. On subsequent

On the Border

mornings, they would break into wide grins at the sight of that tiny creature. Sheenagh would frolic in delight as the soldiers stretched far down to ankle level to greet her and rub her belly. She provided a brief and welcome relief from what I assume would have become a long day during a fraught time.

There were other signs of the October Crisis in the National Capital Region. The celebration of Hallowe'en was cancelled in the village due to security concerns. Jack's father, then the village reeve (or mayor), went on the CBC National News to explain this grave dilemma. There were even tanks on Parliament Hill, God forbid. And I remember having to walk by or around soldiers stationed outside National Defence Headquarters beside my downtown secondary school, Lisgar Collegiate. This might have been routine for children from some troubled countries at our school, but a little unnerving for most of us.

At that time, my father was director of National Historic Sites and Parks. One of the historic parks was Fort Chambly, on the outskirts of Montreal in Pierre Laporte's riding of Chambly. I recall accompanying parents during a trip to Fort Chambly early one Sunday for an official event around the time Mr. Laporte's body was found in the trunk of a car. I remember how eerily quiet it was on that sunny fall occasion. That was a sign of the weeks to come.

In addition to these events, my oldest brother, David, had been studying at Bishop's University in Lennoxville, Québec, until the summer of 1970. He and his wife, Vicki, had just moved to Victoria, BC, when the October Crisis occurred. They remember being shocked at seeing photographs of troops outside the Sherbrooke Armoury near Lennoxville. How could this be happening in their hometown? When my brother and sister-in-law returned to Bishop's for further study a year later, James Cross's daughter was in the same program. My brother and his other fellow students were very conscious and respectful of what the Cross daughter had endured during the Crisis. Prior to his death in Britain in January 2021, Cross had confided that he had never made peace with the event or forgiven his kidnappers, not entirely surprising.

Upon reflection, I'll say the period was a very surreal one. While I have seen much worse during my work and travels abroad, I can only be grateful that our country took a different course from what might have been.

RIDEAU TERRACE CHARADE

Well before Paul Martin Jr. became Canada's twenty-first prime minister, there was his father, Paul Martin Sr. Born in 1904, the latter was a long-time Liberal Party stalwart who served as a member of Parliament during a remarkable thirty-three years in the House of Commons. That doesn't come close to Sir Wilfrid Laurier's forty-four years in Parliament but is still impressive. Martin Sr. served in the cabinets of four different prime ministers and ran unsuccessfully for Canada's highest office on three occasions. So his name was well known to Canadians. He was on the left (quite unlike his right-leaning prime minister son) of a centrist party, particularly in the realm of health care and social benefits. Indeed, he is sometimes referred to as the Father of Medicare. During his last years in political office, Martin Sr. was government leader in the Senate under Prime Minister Pierre Elliott Trudeau. After retirement from politics, he was appointed high commissioner to the United Kingdom, one of Canada's plum diplomatic appointments.

One of the hallmarks of Martin Sr.'s political legacy was his common touch. Early in his political career, when he had more control over his time, he would expend considerable effort visiting his constituents throughout his Windsor Essex-East riding. He prided himself on getting his political intelligence from "the person on the street," like his barber or cab driver. But in the story I am about to relate, these roles were reversed.

In the winter of 1972, our family was living four blocks from where Martin Sr. lived on Rideau Terrace in Ottawa. I was taking driver's education at my downtown secondary school, Lisgar Collegiate, on Monday nights. Although I could easily have hopped on a bus to get there, I preferred to hitchhike. I did so frequently in those days as I enjoyed meeting strangers, as did Martin Sr., it turned out. As chance would have it, he drove downtown on Monday nights for Senate business at the same hour as I would be putting my thumb out. The first time he slowed his long car down to pick me up, Martin Sr. asked me to sit in the back, which I thought a little odd. Was he afraid for his safety? Did he have health problems? Probably neither, as it turned out. I think that Martin Sr. just did not want me to recognize him. The main reason he was offering a ride, I surmised during our times together, was to solicit my views on the Pierre Trudeau government's performance. Martin Sr. likely thought I might bias my responses if I knew who he was. As I was somewhat of a neophyte political junkie, I immediately recognized him but did not let on. Our first conversation ran something like this:

"Come in, young man. Where are you going at this time of night?"

"To Lisgar. I take Driver's Ed on Monday nights," I replied, kicking the snow from my boots as I got in his car.

"Welcome aboard. Do you follow politics?" he inquired directly, peering into the rear-view mirror to see how I would respond.

"Yes, I do actually. I find them interesting. I can't vote yet but I try to follow things." But if the truth be told, my ideas were not well formed or expressed, as the case with most adolescents—and adults, for that matter.

"Do you have a favourite political party?" he enquired, as he turned on the wipers, the snow falling more heavily. Martin Sr. braked slowly to avoid skidding as he came to the corner of Princess Avenue and Sussex Drive outside the governor general's residence, Rideau Hall.

"I like the Liberals. Most of my family does," I replied. In those days I was influenced by my new West Coast brother-in-law, who was an active provincial Liberal Party executive. I found out from my mother years later, however, and much to my surprise, that my father had voted Conservative in every election in which he could vote since his arrival in Canada in 1946.

"That's interesting. I'm a Liberal myself," Martin Sr. remarked. "What do you think about Prime Minister Trudeau? What about his recognition of Red China?"

Many people still referred to the country as Red China to differentiate it from the nationalist Taiwanese government off the east coast. Trudeau was one of the first western leaders to recognize Communist China in 1970. As Martin Sr. was a former minister of foreign affairs, he would have had views on this but he kept them to himself that night.

"Well, change can be difficult," I replied vaguely. "But there are more people in Red China than Taiwan, so it probably makes sense." This issue had resonated at my school as a Taiwanese diplomat's son had circulated a petition opposing Canada's recognition of the Communist regime. My only other indirect knowledge of China in those days related to my purchase of a wonderful set of warm black down Swan Brand mittens from Kwangchow, China which I still have today.

"You seem to be pretty well informed. I am glad to hear that. Where do you get your information?" Martin Sr. enquired as we drove by Ottawa's City Hall.

I was flattered that a major figure in Canadian politics would say this about me but tried to act nonchalant. "Well, I have different sources. I read the *Globe* and listen to the CBC every morning. And talk to my friends and teachers at school."

"That's good," observed Martin Sr. "Have you thought about going into politics? You can do a lot of good there."

"Yes, I have given it some thought. I think politics would be exciting. But I need to finish high school and go to university. And then I need to get elected. A lot could change by then." We both laughed at that.

By this time, we had reached Confederation Square and the old Union Station, which was then not serving much purpose at all. Our conversation came to an end. Martin Sr. suggested I get out at the lights, probably not wanting me to see him turn right onto Parliament Hill. That might have given him away.

Martin Sr. picked me up several more times that winter. He always remembered who I was, even if not by name. We continued our odd charade. He never introduced himself while he probed my views on different contemporary issues like the changes to Canada's immigration policy and Québec separatism.. I pretended that I did not know who he was and answered his questions as honestly as I could. He was courteous and kind in that curious role reversal, where he was the cab driver and I was the passenger.

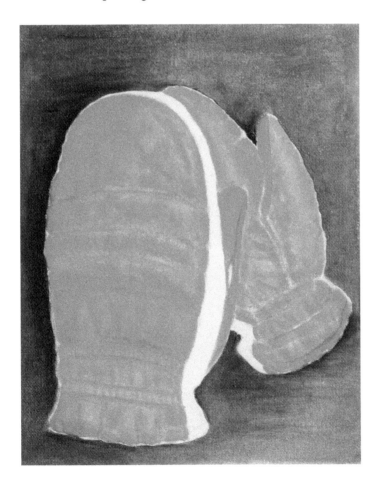

THE SPELL OF THE YUKON

I have had the great fortune to do a lot of exotic and stimulating travel in my time: cloud walking thousands of feet above sea level at mysterious Machu Picchu, Peru; tramping through the myriad temples of Angkor Wat, Cambodia; and swimming through the coral of the Great Barrier Reef, Australia. But one of my best trips and one not as far from home was in the summer of 1974. Years earlier I had completed a school history project on the Klondike Gold Rush of 1898 that piqued my interest. As a result, I had made it one of my young life's ambitions to visit the Klondike, which is close to the Arctic Circle in the Yukon Territory. I had just finished my first year away from home at Queen's University in Kingston, and all that entails—freedom, independence, responsibility, new relationships, and newfound interests. That would be followed by a summer job working near Dawson City, the heart of the Klondike. I would be working in an asbestos mine, which was not everyone's cup of tea due to the known health hazards. But I had developed a sense of adventure and history, largely through my parents, and was keen to set out.

I left Ottawa in late April, a week after exams ended. After being cooped up for a month writing essays and preparing for exams, I was more than ready to go. Following a few nights in Edmonton to finalize my work arrangements with the Chamber of Mines and visit the sister of a friend, I boarded a flight for Whitehorse, the capital of the territory. Flying over the northern Rocky Mountains in late April was spectacular, the snow and ice glinting in the abundant late morning sun. Somehow, things were beginning to feel different. Even the tepid coffee tasted better than it might have otherwise. After brief stops in Grande Prairie, Dawson Creek, and Watson Lake, I arrived in Whitehorse. I had little time for sightseeing but did walk around the small downtown of the city of 12,000 inhabitants before dinner.

The next morning, I boarded a much smaller Northward Airlines plane. Northward no long exists, a victim of the constant upheaval in the Canadian airline industry, particularly for more remote places. The young flight attendant wore a heavy parka, handsewn with Indigenous designs on the back, to protect herself from the sharp blast of cold air at every stop, including Mayo, Keno, and Dawson City. She offered us simple snacks of Dad's Cookies and hot chocolate while providing cheerful and amusing temperature updates. We soon arrived in Clinton Creek, a company town of 430 intrepid souls, where the temperature would dip to minus fifty degrees in the constant dark of winter, although I would not stay that long. Passengers could not get off the plane unless they worked for Cassiar Asbestos

Corporation, my employer. There were no tourist facilities although there was plenty of natural beauty in the surrounding mountains and rivers

Upon boarding a yellow Blue Bird company school bus, I was immediately handed a plasticized industry brochure that refuted in the strongest terms anything I might have heard about asbestos being bad for me. I already knew its perils but was prepared to "suck it up" for one summer (although it turned out to be three). The driver, one of the Johnson brothers who owned the local garage, changed gears expertly at every turn as we snaked our way five miles to the townsite. When we arrived in the townsite, I was immediately struck by the compact, orderly design complete with boardwalks right out of a Western movie. This was a real company town. After being let out at one of the two forty-man bunkhouses, one of which was to be my home for the summer, I unpacked and made my way to the cafeteria across the street for lunch with the other single employees. The few families in town, on the other hand, would cook and consume their own meals at their company-owned home, having purchased the ingredients at the company-run store. The store was so well stocked that the members of the RCMP detachment in nearby Dawson City would make their purchases there. I was not prepared for the massive amounts of cafeteria food required to attract and sustain healthy mineworkers—salad and dessert bars, sandwich tables, a choice of three hot meals, a variety of drinks. I had a large T-bone steak, roast potatoes, corn, salad, and apple pie, a wonderful antidote to the rather pathetic student fare I had consumed all year. As the cafeteria was staffed by professional chefs and served four meals a day, I knew I would not go hungry that summer.

I began work the next day and soon settled into the routine of daily life, enjoying conversing with my coworkers from around the world—France, Indonesia, Australia, and the United States, among other countries. Being surrounded by mountains and two rivers, only just commencing spring ice breakup, was mesmerizing. But the drudgery of shovelling errant asbestos rock and fibre back onto the underground conveyor belt on the way from the mine to the mill was neither healthy nor stimulating. Nor was filling a couple of hundred-pound bags of asbestos a minute in the cavernous mill clouded with asbestos dust. Indeed, a few years later, I began to have disturbing dreams about working in a salt mine, no doubt brought about my experience in Clinton Creek.

During another summer there, one of my responsibilities was ensuring the smooth functioning of the water turbines running the mill and the town sewage plant, the only one in the Yukon at that time. Being the sewage plant operator did not exactly carry great prestige so I did not brag about my work. While not particularly attractive, the environment in the power and sewage plants was at least less of a threat to my health than the thick asbestos dust circulating incessantly in the mill. Surprisingly, that experience proved useful thirty years later when I was responsible for implementing several large municipal water and wastewater treatment plant projects while working in Ottawa for Infrastructure Canada.

What I lived for throughout that first summer, however, was going to Dawson City on my one day off per week, which I seemed to be able to stretch out for longer. I would catch a ride with co-workers into town and stay with an acquaintance of my father's from the Historic Sites, the kind Rev. Ken Snider of St. Paul's Anglican Church, and his young family. Ken and his wife knew everyone in town as well as a great deal about the history of the Klondike so were a great help to me. The tourist town played upon its strengths—its strategic location at the confluence of the Yukon and Klondike rivers, Diamond Tooth Gertie's Gambling Hall (then the only legal casino in Canada!), melodramas at the Palace Grand Theatre, and listening to summer students read the works of the novelist Jack London and bard Robert Service (both writers synonymous with the Klondike) at their respective cabins. I eagerly embraced all those activities. I swore I would go back the next summer and willingly be remunerated much less than at the mine to read Service's epic Klondike ballad *The Cremation of Sam McGee* before spellbound tourists. I didn't do that, unfortunately, as the pay at Clinton Creek was far better and I had to think of helping finance my university education.

I also fancied the hour-long hike from Clinton Creek to the Yukon River, where Forty Mile Village ghost town stood. Established as the first colonists' settlement in the territory in 1886, it once boasted a population of 600 intrepid prospectors and fortune hunters. All that was left by the time I visited were a few wooden structures, a graveyard, and a sadly unkempt apple orchard. But fireweed, the beautiful territorial flower, flourishes during the short growing season when the sun never sets. And across the wide, silty brown Yukon River are the magnificent Ogilvie Mountains. A few lines from Robert Service recall how I felt much of the time when at Forty Mile: "Roaming its giant valley, scaling its god-like peaks; Bathed in its fiery sunsets. . . ." It was an exhilaration occasionally enhanced by a small bottle of Chianti red wine. On a few occasions, I happily swam in the frigid, glacially fed river eddies just to say that I had done so. I did the same thing in the Mackenzie River in the Northwest Territories a few years later.

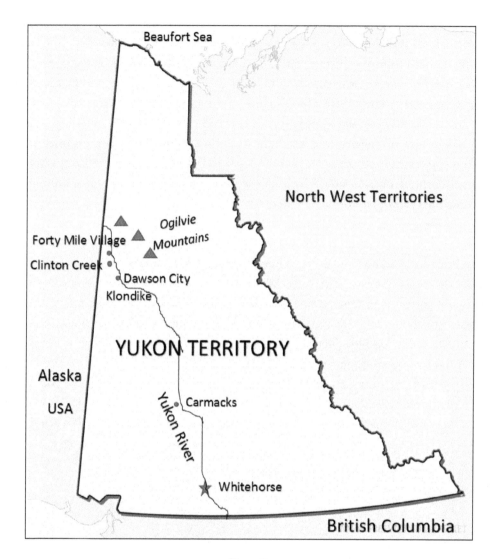

Figure 3

I was fortunate to spend three summers working in the Yukon Territory, Canada, which afforded me superb opportunities to enjoy the wonders of the Yukon, Alaska, and northern British Columbia.

But the greatest of all pleasures began in early August when I left the mine behind. Getting up and eating a light breakfast after a night of major celebration at the community association's Malamute Saloon was not easy, I have to say. I managed to hitch a ride with a company freight truck heading back east to Dawson City. I got out at the junction with of the Top of The World Highway and stuck out my thumb, heading west toward Eagle on the Yukon River, followed by two weeks of exploring the North. I had all that I needed - a backpack, tent, sleeping bag, camp stove, minimal food, and $100 in cash and a few small travellers' cheques. That was meant to last three weeks, including my stays in Vancouver and Victoria with family at the end. It was possible to do that at that time if one lived frugally. Rides were good, with some drivers taking me hundreds of miles and putting me up in their guest bedrooms or basements. And I could not complain if I were sitting beside a wild, fast-flowing river reading a Hermann Hesse novel (popular reading for university students in those days) for an hour or two while waiting for a driver to pick me up. What an incredible sense of solitude and independence!

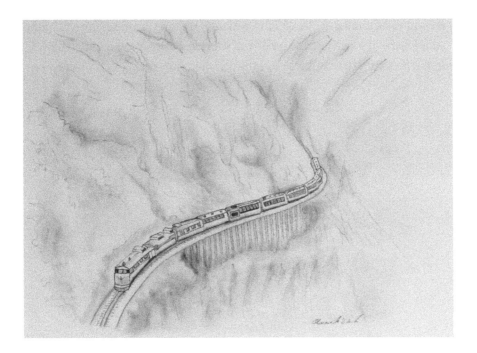

There were various highlights during those three weeks on the road that magic summer. I arrived in the North intoxicated with youth and discovery and drank my fill. I lost track of the wildlife I encountered while hiking in

Mount McKinley (now known as Denali) National Park and had about as many wild blueberries as I could eat. One night I slept inside a beautiful sunlit wood-beamed church near Cordova, Alaska, to avoid a torrential downpour. I revelled in the sound of the falling rain and thunder outside, secure in my blue Woods sleeping bag. I took numerous photos with my father's ancient Zeiss camera while riding the spectacular Yukon-White Pass Railway from Bennett (no relation) Lake to Skagway, Alaska. And marvelled at the massive Columbia Glacier while relaxing on the deck of an Alaska State ferry. Whales and porpoises performed acrobatics for me alone.

I made good friends along the way, many of whom I kept in touch with for a few years. One couple assumed that I was a draft dodger on the run from the continental United States. I was reluctant to put them right, not wanting to spoil the mystery. This was when President Richard Nixon was being impeached after the Watergate conspiracy, a low point in modern American history. Every time we pulled up to a town for lunch or coffee, we would rush to the television to get the latest news. I was elated when Nixon finally resigned from office, the only US president to have done so.

Those were heady days in the summer of '74, which I will not forget. I immersed myself in the natural beauty and history of the North. And I learned much about myself and the generosity of others. I recognize that Robert Service has fallen out of favour, but he might have put it best, I think, when he wrote, "That summer—no sweeter was ever."

NEW YEAR'S DANCE

I was blessed to have parents who had great confidence in me, although it occasionally led to amusing circumstances. Let me explain. I was never more than a slightly above average student either in secondary school or university. That was due partly to the fact that I did not always make maximum effort, always finding other things to occupy my time. My strengths lay more in my contributions to university life. At university I was active in student government and media, promoting the arts, and volunteering with various children's programs in Kingston. When it came to my fourth and final undergraduate year, I was unsure what to do next: travel, graduate studies, government service? It must be said that arts graduates did not have much choice in the matter as their skills were less in demand than those in medicine, engineering, or law, for example. So it was when I headed back to Ottawa for the Thanksgiving weekend that I learned my parents had other ideas. They wanted me to apply for a Rhodes Scholarship and after considerable hesitation, I gave in.

A Rhodes Scholarship is an international postgraduate award for study at the University of Oxford, England. Although the award was first restricted to males from the British Commonwealth as well as the United States and Germany, applicants of both genders from all backgrounds throughout the world can now apply. The purpose is to foster civic-minded leadership and "moral fortitude" (however that might be defined in this day of shifting values) in future leaders regardless of their eventual career paths. Applicants are assessed on both academic merit and other qualities ranging from "courage and kindliness" to commitment to others. Not surprisingly, competition for this award to study at one of the world's best and oldest universities is fierce. Normally less than 1 percent of applicants are successful. Many recipients have gone on to become prominent entrepreneurs, authors, academics, scientists, and politicians.

Why my parents felt I should apply for a Rhodes Scholarship and could be seriously considered is still somewhat unclear to me. I think they may have thought that my contributions to university and town life might play a greater role than my limited scholastic achievement. Or perhaps my parents were trying to live a little vicariously through me. They had left Britain as a young couple with one child in 1943. While they had adapted well to Canada, their chosen home, they clearly missed certain aspects of their familiar British life, like old friends, charming historic towns, and rolling countryside. As my father was an Oxford graduate, he may also have wanted me to have had the same opportunity as him. I recall that he had encouraged me to study at his British private school when I was a few years younger, which I chose not to do. But that's another story.

Upon returning to Kingston at the end of that weekend, I set about applying for the scholarship, a time-consuming and demanding process. I have no idea what rationale or academic pursuit I suggested for my candidacy at Oxford. I did not have any particularly bright suggestions for the focus on my studies regarding settler-Indigenous or federal-provincial relations in Canada, which might have been obvious choices to a Canadian who had studied history and politics such as myself. So, I played up all my extra-curricular contributions, which was all I really could do.

Looking back, I would not want to see what my completed application looked like. I did not have the patience to type accurately so it would have been full of "white out" and mistypes. Readers should remember that this was well before the advent of word processing. Now, even modestly talented individuals like me can churn out something grammatically and typographically correct in a relatively short amount of time. While I did get the required academic referees, I can't help but think they might have supported my candidacy out of friendship or a feeling of obligation as my professors. During this entire process, I felt that there were more qualified candidates and that my efforts would come to naught.

After dutifully submitting my detailed application by registered mail on a cold, bright afternoon at the university post office a few weeks later, the wait began. As I was in arts, I spent much of my time at my student home reading and writing papers or preparing for committee meetings rather than attending the numerous classes and labs of an engineering housemate, for example. And as my bedroom was on the second floor of our rundown Victorian house, I would head downstairs every morning to see whether I had a response to my application when I heard the Canada Post delivery person on the doorstep, second only to our house dog in greeting him.

When I finally got word in early December, the letter arrived in an envelope from a prominent Toronto law firm that was handling the selection process in Canada. As it happened, another law housemate was waiting to learn of an articling job he had applied for and was justifiably mystified why I should get a letter from them. I was embarrassed to have applied for the scholarship and dared not explain. As expected, the letter read something to the effect of "We thank you for your submission but after careful and extensive deliberation, we have determined that there were [many] more qualified candidates. We wish you luck in your future endeavours. . . ." Etcetera. This was the first of several such letters one inevitably gets later in life when applying for jobs and the like.

I have to say that I took the news with both relief at having finished the entire process and a little disappointment. Advising my parents during a Sunday night telephone call home that I had not made the cut went relatively smoothly. What was amusing, however, was a New Year's Day party they hosted a few months later. One of the kind people who supported my application was a close family friend, Denis Coolican. He graciously lamented that the selection committee had obviously not used the right criteria in its deliberations. In earshot, however, was an acquaintance of my parents who happened to be a member of that committee and a former Rhodes Scholar himself. He took umbrage with Denis. A lively debate ensued in which I danced in the middle, trying to defend the perspectives of both people while doing my best not to draw the attention of my parents to our animated discussion. That might have proved fatal in their defence of me. Perhaps this was training to be a diplomat, which was my profession for half my career.

My Rhodes Scholarship application was not something I would have normally chosen to do on my own. Indeed, I am somewhat uneasy as I recount this tale some forty-four years later. But I was lucky that my parents had confidence in me and encouraged me to promote myself at the appropriate time. I also learned that I must go after what I want, an approach that has suited me well throughout my life.

THAT WINTER IN ARIEGE

It was the early winter of 1978. I had graduated from university the previous spring and spent a summer working in an asbestos mine in the Yukon. And then I was off to the University of Dijon (now Burgundy) in France to improve my French. I felt that would be a good idea if I were to seek employment with the federal government. Having spent my formative years in Ottawa observing my parents and other public servants, this seemed entirely logical. And now I was to begin my travels around western Europe, a rite of passage for many of my middle class contemporaries, which I had been eagerly anticipating for years.

It was a mild, sunny Sunday morning in January. The train was headed east from Barcelona, Spain, toward the small town of Foix, the capital of the Ariège department in the French Pyrenees. During my previous few weeks in Spain, I had enjoyed the art and architecture of Seville, Cordoba, and Grenada. I jokingly wondered how my earlier life had been complete without sangria, tapas, and flamenco dance. Now I was headed to the French Pyrenees to visit friends.

The train laboured and the cars clanked. This was not a sleek modern TGV on the Paris-to-Madrid route but an older coach on a tertiary line. Few passengers spoke to each other save in hushed tones to family members or friends. By mid-morning, we were close to the French border. I passed the time in quiet contemplation, recalling an earlier summer with Maurice and Kitty de Bellefeuille on their idyllic mountain farm they called Canton Perdu (or Lost Village). The snowy mountain passes on the border gave way to heavy fog as the train approached Foix. The old abbey and chateau, the main sights of this sleepy town where the Ariège and Arget rivers meet, came into view.

We pulled into the station in an older, semi-industrial part of town. All around were the familiar large and chunky yellow-brown buildings with their high-pitched terracotta roofs. I hauled my brown backpack with its metal frame and crudely sewn maple leaf from the overhead luggage rack. Stuffing the outside pockets with my water bottle, a chocolate bar, guidebook, and map, I checked to make sure I had my old Zeiss camera, a gift from my father. I stepped off the train and saw Maurice just outside the gate carrying his old wicker basket. He was dressed in his usual town attire—blue jeans, work boots, green jacket, and black beret. While he still had his thick grey hair and bushy beard, he was shorter than I remembered. His handshake had lost some of its strength. We walked to the parking lot where the familiar old blue Volkswagen Westfalia van was parked.

"We took the back seats out," Maurice explained, anticipating my question, as he got into the driver's seat, "to transport the honey we have been producing. We've done pretty well at it." I had not enjoyed working with the bees that earlier summer as I was always afraid of being stung, definitely an occupational hazard.

The engine reluctantly turned over, sputtering as it made its usual sewing machine sound. As we turned out of the train station, I asked Maurice whether they still raised rabbits for dinner. I remembered that he would firmly take them from their cages and quickly wring their necks, careful not to prolong the agony.

"No," replied Maurice. "A fox got in a few years ago and devoured them all in short order. We took that as a sign from God that we'd eaten enough rabbits." I smiled as his sarcasm—the de Bellefeuilles were not a religious couple.

My mind wandered back to our weekly trips to Foix on market days. Marcel would do the grocery shopping and run various errands, while I would meander happily on my own through the market and visit various shops—butchers, bakeries, bookstores, and antique dealers. Sometimes I would buy a croissant or large chocolate bar, which I would consume slowly, relishing each bite over the course of the morning. Kitty would stay behind on the farm doing chores but was probably happy to have time on her own.

As we began ascending the mountains, Maurice ground the gears slightly at the hairpin bends. Volkswagen Westfalias had long and awkward gear shifts. In the hamlet of Cautirac just before Canton Perdu, some wiseacre had scrawled *douanes* (customs) on an old piece of cardboard and nailed it to a tree. Tiny and isolated Cautriac seemed about as far from any international border as anyone could imagine although it is not actually that far from Andorra and Spain. This was where Sévrain and Marie lived. He had been a nail maker and had delighted in showing me his exquisitely crafted work. Sévrain once told me about the Guerre de Demoiselles where the inhabitants revolted against the Maître de Forêt, who had unjustly claimed wood from the region for the Crown. Disguised as women, the men hid high in trees, making sinister noises to scare the Maître's officials away from the forest to preserve what little livelihood they had.

Maurice turned right along a long driveway. The old footpath had been cleared of brush and widened, to provide direct access to their house, replacing the circuitous driveway to the back of the property. As we got closer, I saw that the house had been renovated. Wood, glass, and plaster enclosed what was once an open verandah. A new entrance had been added by the parking area. I marvelled at the beauty of the view toward Foix as I breathed in the raw, clean air, exhilarated.

Kitty and I embraced warmly. It was really her that I had come to see. She had been my friend and confidante during that earlier summer. And it had been her with whom I had corresponded over the intervening years. Maurice's unpredictable anger, probably brought about by an inferiority complex and his years as prisoner of war, was not something I had missed at all.

"Welcome. I hope you had a good trip. I've put some coffee on. But you probably want to clean up after your trip," said Kitty as she pulled cookies from the oven and put brown sugar and milk on the table.

"Wonderful. Which bedroom should I use?" I enquired.

"Any of them." So, I chose the one given to me years earlier. Ham radio gears still cluttered the upturned door which served as a desk. Maurice had been a radio operator with the Resistance at the end of World War II. An inflatable Michelin Man that one of the de Bellefeuille boys had obtained years earlier from a gas station stood in the corner, badly in need of air. I had always coveted that relic of years gone by but somehow never managed to obtain one.

After coffee, we caught up on our lives since that first summer. My parents were planning to retire to Victoria after many years in Ontario. Maurice and Kitty's lives had slowed down considerably, both because of their ages and because a farmer's day in winter has a different pace. Kitty was painting more while Maurice had taken up weaving. They spent much of their days in silent communion, which I found a little odd. Their children were all doing graduate work in fields I couldn't really grasp.

After the long train ride, I needed exercise. So, after a quick lunch of soup, cheese, and bread, I set out to visit Sévrain and Marie back in Cautirac. As I walked along the driveway, I thought of the times that Kitty had sent me to see them with a basket of freshly picked berries as an offering so I could practise my limited French. Although understandably wizened over the years and missing a few more teeth, Sévrain and Marie were much the same, a devoted couple living simply on their small government pension in an isolated mountain village. One of their few concessions to modernity was a bright neon light in the kitchen. Sadly, it detracted from the rustic atmosphere of their cozy old stone house.

"How is the outside world?" enquired Sévrain, grinning as he poured me a strawberry liqueur.

"Well, a lot has changed since I was last here. Where do you want me to begin?" I replied, grinning at the enormity of the question. We chatted about various things while I basked happily in front of the glowing fire. Marie was keen that their little hamlet replace their water supply due to suspected well contamination. Their lives were much different from mine, although not free from worry or challenge either. We city dwellers tend to romanticize the rural lifestyle.

After saying farewell, I returned to Canton Perdu, where I leafed through some of the books I had read years earlier, including Saul Bellow's *Herzog* and a Graham Greene novel. Slightly ambitious reading for a fourteen-year-old, I reflected. After dinner, we spoke of Maurice's old Résistance friend, François. I had found it amusing that his partner was conveniently named Françoise. A psychiatrist, he had been on national TV the night before talking about a new theory he was promoting.

Early the next morning, Kitty knocked on my door, talking excitedly about the view from the living room window. Reluctant as I was to get out of my warm bed, I made my way to the living room and was struck by the sight. Wispy, multi-coloured stratus clouds eked their way west into the mountain slopes. Banks of low-lying, thick clouds hung heavily over the patchwork rolling farms to the centre, freshly blanketed with snow. The odd building jutted up from under. Still further, Foix, with its normally imposing chateaux and rivers, was nowhere to be seen. And higher in the sky, the sun was tentatively breaking through with the promise of a beautiful day. Kitty and I sat silently, sipping our coffee, marveling at this spectacle.

But the weather changed and by late morning, it was snowing heavily. As I love snowfalls no matter where I am, I decided to go for a walk. I packed a lunch of pâté, bread, apples, and a flask of the red wine Maurice purchased by the keg in Montpelier. I trudged north of Canton Perdu further into the mountains, hoping to find an old trail we had taken during one of our frequent summer afternoon excursions picking mushrooms. Duck with *girolles* (a local mushroom), butter, and parsley had been one of Kitty's specialties.

Without snowshoes or cross-country skis, I soon found myself calf-deep in snow and making slow progress. That was of little concern to me as I savoured this winter paradise. I passed several stone and wood farm buildings bursting with winter fodder and deserted old shepherds' shelters built into the mountain sides. The powdered snow on the birch trees fell gently to the ground under its own weight or with a gust of wind. Hare tracks crisscrossed the trail. I forded small black creeks not yet frozen and delighted in the sound of running water.

My hunch was correct, and I soon found myself in another remote and nearly abandoned village, les Spéyrous. An older woman leaned out of the window while beating a worn carpet. A large German Shepherd barked out a warning of my arrival.

"Bonjour! I'm from Canada," I began. "I remember you from when I stayed on the de Bellefeuille farm a few years ago. I've been studying in Dijon and am back for a short visit."

"Well, I'm pleased to see you again. Please give my regards to Mme. et M. de Bellefeuille. We never see them here. There's no direct route between these villages, as you know."

After a few more pleasantries, I took my leave and continued my trek. Eventually, I found another trail, which I knew would take me to a deserted mill along a small rushing river, where I hungrily ate my lunch. I made my way back to Canton Perdu in time for late afternoon tea and shortbread with Kitty and Maurice. I had recently taken a course in French politics so was keen to impress them with my newfound knowledge. They were not happy about the Communist Party's recent decision to return to the Soviet orbit once again. Maurice's memories of an authoritarian regime were too fresh to think otherwise.

I spent much of that evening reading, journaling, and writing the postcards I had collected in Spain. I retired early to prepare for the train trip to Montpelier to meet up with my old friend and travelling companion, Jack, who had been studying in Montpellier. I had enjoyed my return to the mountains and was sad to leave Kitty and Maurice. To my disappointment, they were to separate only a few years later. He moved to Brittany, where he could sail all afternoon with his new partner. Kitty remained on the farm until moving to a seniors' home in Montpellier. She was a gentle, kind soul. I saw her only a few more times before her death. My love of France and travel was largely engendered by the experience of my first summer with Maurice and Kitty at Canton Perdu.

WHEN IN OTTAWA

Throughout the course of my life, I have had the opportunity to dine at a variety of cafeterias, including those at penny-pinching schools and universities, idyllic children's summer camps, rough-and-ready mining towns, gracious art galleries and museums, and drab federal government office buildings. They have all had their strengths and weaknesses but the one I remember most was at External (now Global) Affairs Canada in Ottawa. Given that I had lunch and coffee there almost daily for seven years over a thirteen-year period, I consider myself somewhat of an expert on that one.

By way of background, External Affairs is the Canadian federal government department responsible for international relations, as the name suggests. The department has an illustrious history (for Christian white men, at least, due to prevailing social norms) and entry into its hallowed halls has always been a highly prized career path for university graduates, although the sheen has come off in recent years for reasons I shall not get into here. Notable denizens in its early years included O. D. Skelton, Lester Pearson, Norman Robertson, and Hume Wrong. As these diplomats spent considerable time abroad, they became accustomed to finer dining and would likely be disappointed in the culinary fare upon their return to Ottawa. Unfortunately, Ottawa's miserable food reputation did not begin to improve until the 1980s. The nation's capital was becoming more cosmopolitan with the influx of more immigrants from diverse cultures and greater world travel by its citizens. The latter would demand more than Kraft Dinner or well-done roast beef and mashed potatoes upon their return from abroad.

When I joined External Affairs in 1982, the department had finally moved from various dingy and crowded buildings around the National Capital Region to the much-vaunted Lester B. Pearson Building. It had a premier location along sedate Sussex Drive, close to the French Embassy and the Official Residences of the prime minister and governor general. The new building, however, was not to everyone's taste, including mine. Described by some as a "chocolate box," the Canadian Register of Historic Places dispassionately suggests that it is "an excellent illustration of the late Modern Movement in architecture, with the influence of *brutalism*" (*my emphasis*). Who but an iconoclast could admit to being a fan of something called brutalism? Throughout my years in the department, I found the building to be dark, depressing, and thoroughly lacking in soul. I note that it is currently undergoing much-needed renovation and hope that the revised version will be a lot brighter, inviting, and conducive to creativity.

One exception to my rather bleak aesthetic assessment of the building was the cafeteria. Located in a naturally well-lit and spacious area in Tower D, which was not a tower where you wanted to be in those days from a career perspective. Its occupants were generally engaged in various administrative and staffing functions, considered inferior by many to the more pressing foreign policy pursuits being carried out by those in the other three towers.

What happened in the cafeteria itself is what I am more interested in, however. In my view, the comportment of diners might be said to have mirrored the pattern of the life of the department or individual career trajectories, as in my case, perhaps. Contacts and decisions were often made over *coq au vin* or Friday's *brook trout meunière*. Given the cafeteria's role in these developments, I have been trying to figure out the right metaphor to use in describing this place. Might it be Brussels on the Rideau, shark tank, or even sewer? Perhaps you can help.

Let's begin with Brussels on the Rideau, perhaps the most positive and apt of the metaphors. Brussels, Belgium, is renowned for its cuisine, which is often compared favourably with French food. Its waffles, beer, chocolate, and French fries have an excellent international reputation. So, too, was the Pearson Building cafeteria once held in high esteem (as far as government cafeterias were concerned, at least). In fact, some counterparts in other departments would schedule their meetings to take advantage of the opportunity to have a meal there. Sadly, the quality of its offerings had declined precipitously within a decade, so that many members of the department chose to microwave the remains of the previous night's meal or assemble sandwiches from home to consume in their own offices. Or just go out for a long walk.

We need to explore this possible metaphor further. In those halcyon days when we thought we were going to change the world (what persons who grew up in the '60s did not aspire to do so?), we engaged in passionate meal-time discussions on a wide range of weighty topics (or at least they were to us). This was perhaps not unlike the multilateral meetings of the two august international bodies based in Brussels: NATO (the North Atlantic Treaty Organization) and the European Community, the latter in its early incarnation before being bogged down by bureaucracy and emasculated by nationalist sentiment, in the view of its detractors. But the privileged position once held by External Affairs had been largely eclipsed by the prime minister's office and other departments by the late-'80s. Our mealtime discussions began to focus on the loss of prestige and benefits or lack of career progress. Indeed, an internal foreign service officer listserv called E-Whine was created in the 90s to do just that. The moniker says it all with regard to staff morale.

Finally, the building itself is located on the Rideau River, one of three rivers in the Ottawa area. The growth of the pre-capital settlement (Bytown) was predicated upon the harvesting of local forests as part of the timber industry. Similarly, Brussels is also host to a river, the Senne (not be confused with the more romantic and better-known Seine in Paris), which was largely filled in during the eighteenth and nineteenth centuries in the course of urban development; thus, both shared less illustrious industrial pasts.

What about the shark tank metaphor, where sharks voraciously feed upon the younger, weaker, or less efficient of the smaller species? The department, like most workplaces, was a place where personal power and privilege seemed to be exercised and demonstrated in such simple ways as where employees sat in relation to others while having lunch. Junior diplomats ensconced themselves on the long table to the front left of the cash registers, eager to be seen and observe departmental rituals but oblivious to the fate that awaited many of them. Those who had made it to ten years or more but had not been promoted sat to the left and beyond the juniors at small, square tables in groups of two or three. They were still eager to contribute and advance but not sure how to do so, or if indeed that was at all possible. Here, there would be many long faces the day the promotion lists came out. Immigration officers, who had only recently joined the department and were never fully accepted by many traditional foreign service officers, had their own tables. Non-foreign service officers including support staff sat scattered unobtrusively where they could, not consumed by the same competition to survive.

What of the sewer metaphor? When I became a diplomat, External Affairs was amalgamating three different departments with overseas mandates: Immigration, Trade, and the traditional Department of External Affairs. The descriptor often given to this process was "three different streams leading to one common river," but I coined the term "three different streams leading to one common sewer." This was because the experience with the amalgamation process was extremely negative for some. It created dissatisfaction among traditional diplomats ensconced in their ways and led to frequent internecine friction over the years. And did anyone learn from this experience? I suspect not, as the department has reinvented itself several time since then, as is inevitable in all organizations. This metaphor is a little disgusting perhaps but one that appeals to me as I was once responsible for the efficient functioning of a town sewage plant in the Yukon Territory. I also subsequently negotiated and managed wastewater plant projects at Infrastructure Canada.

I am not sure why all metaphors I have suggested relate to water. Is water the giver of life, as some religions or philosophies contend, or are we all being flushed downstream? I hope the reader can appreciate that several of these metaphors can be applied to the cafeteria. Selecting the most appropriate depends on one's working experience at External Affairs and views on organizational behaviour generally. Take your pick (or plunger). I can only say that I was happy to have left External Affairs years ago to get on with a more normal life and be free to eat what I wanted for lunch and have greater control over the circumstances in which I did.

DONG KHOI STROLL

Today's visitors to Ho Chi Minh City (formerly known as Saigon) experience a sprawling, noisy, and chaotic place. Most observers agree that it has less charm than its northern sister and the capital of Vietnam, Hanoi. Nonetheless, tourists, businesspeople, and returning overseas Vietnamese flock to Ho Chi Minh City to take in its many sounds and sights. The wartime history is played up, although from a Communist perspective. A visit to the War Remnants Museum is essential while a Mekong River cruise is highly recommended. Consumer goods are ubiquitous and night life abounds. Honking cars veer out of nowhere. Merely crossing the street on foot can be life threatening. Many of the locals you are likely to meet speak at least a little English.

But it wasn't always so. In the autumn of 1983, eight years after the "fall" (or "liberation," as the Communist government likes to say) of The Republic of South Vietnam, I had the rare opportunity to travel to Ho Chi Minh City from Bangkok, Thailand. I was assigned as a third secretary at the Canadian Embassy on my first foreign posting. Canada had signed a family reunification accord with the Vietnamese government, and I was in Ho Chi Minh City to interview candidates who had been granted exit permits by the Vietnamese, subject to meeting Canadian immigration requirements. That I was exhilarated to be there was an understatement. I felt I was living history. This was the Saigon that had so dominated the news for much of my childhood and teenage years because of the tragic Vietnam War. *The Deer Hunter*, an epic American war film that partly takes place in Saigon, had piqued my interest several years earlier. Indeed, I was fortunate to meet one of the bit actors by chance while living in Bangkok just prior to my first trip to Vietnam.

During the short flight from Thailand, I was struck by the fact that the weekly Air France flight was virtually empty, with only a few aid workers, UN officials, French businessmen, foreign employees of Vietnamese co-operatives, and diplomats such as myself. I arrived at Tan Son Nhất Airport (once the busiest military airbase in the world), where I witnessed hundreds of Vietnamese gathering excitedly to see off their family members, friends, and neighbours. They were the lucky ones, departing for new lives in Canada, France, the United States, and Australia, the four countries accepting the greatest number of Vietnamese immigrants. They were legally fleeing decades of colonial rule, war, and communism, unlike others who desperately took to the sea to escape the new regime. The "others" were the Boat People, thousands of whom were raped, robbed, killed, or never heard from again.

I was staying at the Cuu Long ("Nine Dragons" in Vietnamese) Hotel, a grand if somewhat dilapidated art deco riverfront structure built in 1929 on Dong Khoi Street, Ho Chi Minh City's best-known thoroughfare. The Cuu Long was one of the few hotels catering to foreigners during the early years of the Communist government. The lobby was an awkward hexagonal shape, and the walls and ceilings were different shades of off-white. The shiny, brown angular chairs and sofas had clearly not been replaced since the departure of the Americans and gave the lobby a retro '60s look. The deserted bar was off to the left and hidden from the street by thick foliage separating the hotel from the sidewalk. I would later have an occasional evening aperitif there before heading to a restaurant with colleagues.

Hotel porters hovered, keen to carry my baggage, hopeful they would be rewarded with a package of 555 cigarettes. They could sell that on the black market for the equivalent of a month's wages. Tipping with actual money, particularly American dollars, was a sign of a decadent capitalist economy and, consequently, prohibited. The narrow elevator had been installed during the American years and had not been serviced by an authorized representative since before 1975, so using it at all was a calculated gamble. But its unpredictable operation reassured me that I was not staying in a well-functioning but anonymous Holiday or Ramada Inn in some non-descript Canadian city.

I was booked in one of the spacious fourth-floor staterooms overlooking the Saigon River, where I soon learned to relax in relative splendour after countless and exhausting immigration interviews each day. I appreciated the extra space, traditional lacquerware art and furniture, relative quiet, and functioning air conditioning, so necessary in the humid climate. After unpacking and showering, I returned to the lobby and made my way to the reception, where Chau was on duty. She was dressed in an *ao dai*, the traditional women's tight-fitting silk tunic worn over black pants. Like everyone in the service industry in Vietnam, Chau was poorly paid but at least had work. That was significant given the severe unemployment from which Vietnam suffered but would not admit. That would be tantamount to acknowledging that the Communist system, over which the long war in Vietnam had been fought, was not working.

I stepped outside onto Dong Khoi and was immediately struck by the heat and humidity. This was the rainy season. There had been record flooding, which had brought hordes of rats from the north, according to some. I was accosted by several cyclo drivers clamouring, "You need cyclo?" and "Where you go, Canada?" How did they know where I was from? I had only just arrived. Their three-wheeled rickshaw taxis were a cheap and pleasant way to get around. Now, of course, drivers charge more due to their rarity and the bustling nature of the city. Many of the drivers then were former Army of the Republic of (South) Vietnam soldiers required to work as informants in the service of the Communist government after the war. So, one had to be careful where one went and what one said, but the upside was that the drivers knew the city well. They could usually speak passable English, which was uncommon in those days.

As there were no cars, locals were able to cycle freely along Dong Khoi, which was lined with cafes and lacquerware shops. Many of these were unofficial money changers who would swap American dollars for us at thirty times the official rate. So why would you go to the government bank to do this? To my immediate left of the hotel was Maxim's, a garish, upscale restaurant with live music, private rooms, and wonderful seafood. A few well-to-do emigrants would hold lavish celebratory farewell dinners there.

Business on Dong Khoi was slow that day (and every day for that matter). *Lien so* (Russians) had no money to spend and there were few Westerners, except those in some official capacity, such as myself. Everywhere were photographs of Ho Chi Minh, the nationalist revolutionary leader who brought the Communists to power in North Vietnam prior to unification in 1975. Known affectionately as "the father of the country," Ho was usually depicted with a greying beard, dressed in simple loose clothes, often playing with children, someone you might invite for dinner. I stopped for an excellent café *filtre* and *croissant*, reminders of Vietnam's French colonial past. Young children approached selling peanuts for ten *dong*, less than a pittance for me but a small fortune to them. Some were of mixed race, the children of French or American soldiers or issue from the sex trade. Life for the *bui doi*, or "dust of life," as they were called, was grim.

As I walked away from the river toward Lam Son Square, there was more activity. At this, the most impressive civic *carrefour* in Ho Chi Minh City, French colonial architecture could be seen everywhere. On my immediate right was the Caravelle Hotel, then known as the Doc Lap (Independence). It was built of Italian marble and later reinforced with bullet-proof glass as the war progressed and security deteriorated. The hotel became home to various embassies and media outlets prior to 1975 and served as the setting for much of the excellent 2002 film version of Graham Greene's *The Quiet American*.

Old Post Office, Ho Chi Minh City

Kitty-corner from the Caravelle was the grand Municipal Theatre, which also once served as the Opera House. And across the street from that was the Continental Hotel, then unoccupied and run-down. It had been the centre of French colonial life in South Vietnam. Across Dong Khoi and diagonally opposite the Caravelle stood the Rex Hotel, which, oddly enough, began life as a car dealership and garage but was refashioned into a hotel and cultural centre. It was the busy site of the American Military Command's daily briefings until 1975. In the early years of the Communist regime, a very bizarre ritual would take place at the Rex on Saturday nights. This was a country where the traditional dynamics between classes had been upended and where contact between locals and foreigners was normally discouraged except in an official capacity. Yet foreigners were permitted to dance at the Rex with young Vietnamese women dressed in traditional *ao dai* for the equivalent of one dollar. Everything was strictly "on the up and up," however. Asking the women out for a drink afterward was not tolerated. These women had been thoroughly vetted for their allegiance to the regime by the appropriate authorities and were likely gathering intelligence while carrying out their duties.

I could happily spend hours around Lam Son Square at any time of day. In the early morning, stooped old women would sweep the sidewalk with large brooms. Others set up their cigarette stands where they would sell their wares individually rather than by the package, which few could afford. Some would hawk *xoi,* steamed rice with soya beans and sweet corn or peanuts. I could make out the rhythmic tapping of bamboo sticks by small boys announcing the approach of a *pho* cart. A photographer would set up his outdoor studio. An old grey bus with screeching, worn axles occasionally went by, spewing black exhaust and tilting badly under the weight of its passengers.

I would also visit the nearby neighbourhoods and thoroughfares in the early evening. Children playing happily on the sidewalk, with the simplest of toys or games. The busy street vendors selling tasty *cha gio* and other Vietnamese dinner specialties. Hundreds of bicycles, some carrying enormous loads, meeting chaotically at inter-sections but somehow never colliding. There were strolling lovers, holding hands, impervious to the world around them, a timeless and universal tradition. I remember joyful family celebrations, perhaps graduations or weddings. And the burning of joss sticks as an offering to ancestors in the dim evening light brought about by the frequent power outages.

But it would be naïve to suggest that Ho Chi Minh City was all romance, beauty and happiness. Underneath a thin veneer was great oppression and deprivation. It seemed as if most of the people I spoke with were keen to leave the country. I was often importuned by acquaintances desperate for me to carry letters abroad (avoiding the official censors) or to bring back dollars from relatives abroad. During one of my evening strolls, I turned left at Ngo Duc Ke Street and headed toward Nguyen Hue, a grand boulevard one block over from Dong Khoi. I passed rows of red-finned American cars, which sat idle most of the time. They were occasionally rented for special events like weddings, a curious and contradictory testament to the American war-time presence. Many homeless families and single men, likely having migrated illegally from the provinces or committed some minor offence against the regime, lay sleeping in the dark at various points along the dark sidewalk. They were prey to mosquitos, cockroaches, and rats, as well as interrogation or worse by the local authorities. The new regime had not been kind to everyone.

On another occasion, I was sitting in a nearby restaurant having dinner with a colleague. I became conscious of a middle-aged homeless man in tattered clothing with no shoes positioning himself above an open manhole. His chin was bristly and his hair unkempt. His shirt was army green, perhaps a castoff from a soldier. Or maybe he had been a soldier himself. He removed his worn trousers and crouched, preparing to defecate, with no apparent concern at being seen by passersby or the restaurant's clientele. And what did it matter to this man, anyway? He had been ignored by the new Vietnam and owed society nothing. The reality was that there were few public washrooms in Ho Chi Minh City and the man had no paper or water to clean himself afterward. Shortages in Vietnam were chronic—of food, medicine, human rights, and hope. These shortages persist for many even today, particularly in the countryside.

But from my privileged perspective, I loved Ho Chi Minh City as it was then—the colonial architecture, the cadence of the spoken language, the warmth of the people, the wonderful combination of Vietnamese, Chinese, and French food, the brief, intense afternoon showers, the springtime flowers, the excitement of youth, the intensity of work . . . I did return many years later as a tourist and was inevitably disappointed. Can one ever go back and hope things will be the same? But my memories of that magical first trip will remain with me forever.

Figure 4

I conducted refugee interviews at Khao-I-Dang on the Cambodian border and in Saigon from 1983-1985.
I also served as an UNTAC International Pilling Station Office in Prey Veng Province, Cambodia in 1993.

ON THE BORDER

In the spring of 1975, the governments of Vietnam, Laos, and Cambodia (collectively known sometimes as French Indochina) fell under Communist control. That brought an end to decades of colonial rule, national liberation struggles, Marxist-Leninist internecine conflict and American dominance and mythic invincibility in Southeast Asia. While Vietnam and Laos came within the Soviet orbit, Cambodia largely pursued its own path, albeit with considerable support from China. Although the American-backed regimes in power until 1975 had been problematic and could not have been described as democratic, those that assumed control in April 1975 engaged in severe abuses of political power. They proved themselves ready to entirely suppress human rights and lives in their attempts at profound social and economic restructuring.

The most brutal of all was Pol Pot's genocidal Khmer Rouge regime in Cambodia (also known as Kampuchea) from 1975 to late 1978. During its reign of terror, the Khmer Rouge introduced a systematic program of religious persecution, extermination of ethnic minorities, and forced relocation of urban dwellers to the countryside to begin a disastrous utopian agrarian revolution. Although estimates vary considerably, the general consensus is that up to 20 percent of the population of 7.3 million was exterminated while two million were displaced. When a Vietnamese-backed force finally invaded Cambodia in December 1978 to install a puppet regime favourable to them, 2.5 million Cambodians were at risk of starvation. Although the Vietnamese were initially welcomed by some, their occupation soon alienated much of the population.

As the nature of the Communist regimes became clear and the human toll mounted, the exodus from French Indochina accelerated. That which garnered most public attention was the plight of 700,000 Vietnamese Boat People, who attempted perilous sea journeys to Hong Kong, the Philippines, Malaysia, and elsewhere. Equally shocking, however, was the unexpected arrival of 750,000 starving, malnourished, and traumatized Cambodians along the Thai border from a country about which little was known. The West had no comprehension of the scale of the brutality and suffering of the Cambodian population due to the almost total news blackout from the isolated Khmer Rouge regime. This was well before the days of CNN and the 24 hour news cycle.

As the flow of refugees from these three countries continued, more became known about conditions in these three countries. Excellent popular books and movies were soon produced that proved helpful in sensitizing the world to these grim new realities. These included Stanley Karnow's *Vietnam: A Television History*, William Shawcross's *Sideshow: Kissinger, Nixon and the Destruction of Cambodia* and *The Killing Fields* with the actor Sam Waterston as the American journalist, Sydney H. Schanberg.

After some hesitation and debate, the Thai government, donor and resettlement countries, the United Nations, and various humanitarian organizations swung into action on a massive scale to deal with the influx of Cambodian refugees. The small Thai-Cambodian border town, Aranyaprathet (known also as Aran), which served as an accommodation and logistical hub, was overwhelmed. Khao-I-Dang (KID) refugee camp, co-managed by the United Nations High Commissioner for Refugees and the Thai government and army, was established in 1979. Twenty kilometres north of Aran, KID was unique as the sole camp not controlled by one of the Cambodian Non-Communist resistance forces. These forces included the Khmer People's National Liberation Front of former Premier Son Sann and a faction led by Prince Norodom Sihanouk, Cambodia's head of state prior to the Khmer Rouge regime. Khao-I-Dang inhabitants (unlike those in other camps) were eligible for highly sought-after resettlement to third countries such as Canada, Australia, France, and the United States. Designed to accommodate up to 100,000 people (enormous in those days), the camp population overflowed to 160,000 in March 1980. When I undertook my immigration selection trips from 1983 to 1985, however, the population was around 40,000 refugees.

Camp conditions were very mixed. There is no doubt that the refugees were physically safer in KID than elsewhere along the border or often in Cambodia itself. They also had access to food, water, and shelter. Some additional services were soon offered to the refugees, many of which they might not have been able to enjoy in Cambodia, including traditional Khmer and western medicine, basic education, and language training. Indeed, conditions in the camp were often better than in the surrounding Thai villages (which is not saying a whole lot), leading to some jealousy and friction. On the other hand, KID and other border camps were often overcrowded and the inhabitants subject to theft and extortion by Cambodian bandits and Thai soldiers. The latter were paid poorly and thus could not entirely be blamed for trying to take advantage of the unexpected situation. Finally, camp residents lived a life circumscribed by regulations and barbed wire fences and were often subject to harsh and arbitrary Thai army justice.

Throughout the existence of the border camps (including KID), there was considerable discussion as to what should be done with the refugees. Possible "durable" or long-term solutions included resettlement abroad to countries such as Canada, integration with the local Thai population, or repatriation to Cambodia if and when conditions there improved. There was concern that refugees were losing their self-reliance, living too long in conditions where services were being provided to them. Some Thais knowledgeable about the situation, including several Embassy employees, felt the refugee population to be an enormous burden and could not understand why resettlement countries such as Canada were willing to accept them.

It was in this context that I was tasked by Canada's Department of External Affairs (now Global Affairs Canada) with interviewing Cambodian, Vietnamese, and Laotian refugees in all the Thai refugee camps for immigration to Canada. During my two years at the embassy, I undertook approximately twenty refugee camp trips. After doing the exhausting interviews, I would make it a point to have a guided tour of camps with appropriate officials to get a better sense of conditions. And as more of my selection trips were to KID than to the Vietnamese or Laotian camps, I became particularly interested in and relatively knowledgeable about developments along the border.

The candidates for immigration to Canada had obviously come from very dire circumstances, so it was difficult not to feel sincere compassion for their plight; but at the same time, I had to uphold the laws and regulations of Canada's immigration program. If the truth be told, many of these had been formulated very quickly given the extraordinary and rapidly evolving circumstances on the ground. This meant that visa officers such as me often had significant leeway in their interpretation of them. It was also, in some ways, a blessing that I had no previous immigration experience and inadequate preparation (for reasons I will not go into here) in Ottawa prior to my departure. As a result, I was not as rigid or jaded as I might otherwise have been in my work, which was sometimes the case with veteran visa officers.

These were far from normal immigration interviews. How do you interview people whose lives had been torn asunder, whose education had been interrupted, who had lost all their possessions, or whose family members had been deliberately separated, executed, or disappeared? Still others had lost a lower limb while crossing the heavily land-mined border to reach sanctuary and their family in KID. Their prosthetic was often skillfully and ingeniously fabricated by other refugees from spare wood, metal and old automobile tires. Most of those we met were semi-literate farmers with large families and no relevant work experience. Few could speak English or French, as the Khmer Rouge had forbidden teaching or speaking these languages, which they interpreted as symbols of a corrupt and capitalist West. In light of these challenges, how would these refugees be able to adapt and contribute to Canada's modern, increasingly urban and competitive environment, we had to ask ourselves. Most had never used a phone or ridden in a car. Had they been active members of the Khmer Rouge and helped perpetrate some of Pol Pot's atrocities? We had little way of assessing this possibility due to the dearth of available information. As visa officers, we did not want to be called to appear before the Deschênes Commission of Inquiry on War Criminals in Canada, which was deliberating at that time, for having unknowingly admitted a war criminal.

With each interview, we did not know what had happened the night before. Had they been subject to beatings or jail by Thai authorities for operating a small store to supplement their meagre lifestyle? Had they succeeded in getting their older cousin, for example, from whom they had been separated years earlier during the forced migration from Phnom Penh to the countryside, into the camp? For Cambodians, the notion of responsibility to family was far more important than for the average Canadian. But one of Canada's immigration priorities was reuniting such families.

There was little the candidates could do to prepare for our interviews except dress as best as they could (often in their one change of tattered clothes), ensure that all family members were present and rehearse a few lines of broken English that they probably did not understand. They would often be prompted in how to respond the night before by their fellow refugees who would also serve as volunteer interpreters during the interviews. Although normal immigration procedures require the submission of extensive documentation, this was not the case in KID. Due to the refugees' rapid flight from Cambodia and given the limited level of literacy in Cambodia, there were few or no documents to be readied. Some candidates did, however, obtain letters from the organizations with which they volunteered in the camp to demonstrate their initiative and potential ability to adapt to Canada.

The days were long, sweaty, and exhausting. The interviews were held at an old school between Aran and KID with no running water and only sporadic electricity to run portable fans. We were sometimes double booked with other resettlement countries, which proved frustrating as we wanted to ensure that we completed our scheduled interviews while the refugees had permission to exit the camp for the day. After dinner there was little to do in the normally quiet Aran. One American colleague who carried out interview pre-screening tried to remedy this situation by hiring a motorcycle and driver to travel across the border into Cambodia after dark. She wanted to see how far she could get before being stopped by bandits or rebel armed factions. Against my better judgement, I accompanied her a short distance on one occasion but decided that was not for me.

Surprisingly, I loved those trips to KID. I was given responsibility far beyond my experience and knowledge. As visa officers, we developed a great camaraderie amongst ourselves, as one often does in challenging circumstances. And I was moved by the close-knit families sitting before me recounting their harrowing experiences. I learned more about Buddhism, Southeast Asia, and overcoming adversity than I could have dreamt. Every night I would eat dinner with colleagues and contacts from the varied refugee-focused community, exchanging experiences and intelligence. Then I would retire to my hotel room to read more Shawcross—perhaps *The Quality of Mercy: Cambodia, Holocaust and Modern Conscience*. I have always liked the way his publishers chose his book titles—succinct and deliberate.

Canada distinguished itself early on in its response to the flight of the Cambodians, Laotians, and Vietnamese. Cabinet ministers at the highest level signalled their commitment, legislation was drafted, agreements were made with other levels of government, sponsors were found, and visa officers were deployed to the field, all in short order. From 1979 to 1980, Canada accepted 60,000 Indochinese refugees, which represented 25 percent of our immigration total for those years. Public sentiment toward and mobilization on behalf of Indochinese refugees was incredibly positive, as exemplified by the City of Ottawa's Project 4,000. This initiative was undertaken when then-Mayor Marion Dewar committed to sponsoring 4,000 Vietnamese Boat People in addition to the 4,000 Canada had already accepted by 1979.

Over three decades, Canada accepted 202,000 Indochinese refugees, an unprecedented figure compared with any other previous Canadian refugee intake. It also compared favourably with the other three major resettlement countries. Our innovative action in permitting the private sponsorship of refugees by churches and schools set the groundwork for future refugee movements to Canada and an example to other resettlement countries. Canada's extraordinary efforts were recognized by the UNHCR when it presented "the people of Canada" with its 1986 Nansen Refugee Award for its efforts on behalf of the forcibly displaced from Indochina and other situations.

I would be remiss if I did not recognize the enormous contributions of the Cambodians, Laotians, and Vietnamese to Canada since their arrival in fields such as science, business, sports, and the arts. Indeed, a Laotian Canadian, Souvankham Thammavongsa, who was born in one of the Thai camps, won the 2020 Scotiabank Giller Prize, Canada's most important annual award for a novel or short story collection. Vietnamese-Canadian Carol Huynh became a successful Olympic athlete.

This has been the most difficult life story to write in this collection because it brings back many mixed emotions. I had many disparate strings to tie together as I collected my thoughts. My days along the border are ones I will never forget. I am immensely proud to have to been able to respond in my small way to a massive crisis brought on by an extraordinary set of dramatic circumstances.

ESPRESSO AT LANGANO

We are woken early by the cacophony of birds and insects. It would be hard to get tired of that kind of hardship. Egyptian geese, flying pelicans, silver cheeked hornbills, fish eagles, and white flying cranes populate the coastline here, swooping while searching for prey, each with their distinctive cries or songs, crest and circle. Large male cicadas with their eyes spread apart issue their loud, shrill droning noise in the long, dry grass surrounding the cottage. Geckos dart across the short sandy path to the deserted beach under the wedding-like canopy of acacia trees. A large indigo lizard hides in the shadows, waiting for breakfast to fly by.

Anna gets up silently to make the first morning espresso with the sleek silver Bialetti, followed by a tasty omelette with the few eggs purchased from local children after our arrival late yesterday afternoon. She is wearing a simple white T-shirt and has her hair pulled back with an elastic band saved from the last bundle of carrots we bought at our neighbourhood market in Addis. I stumble to the bathroom in my old plaid boxer shorts and black flip flops to do my teeth—if I have remembered my brush, that is. We were keen to leave the city and return to this paradise so we packed in a hurry. I spy a dead mouse in the trap by the garbage can. Kevin, who just turned six, has been up for ages, happily playing with the wooden toy trains he got from a friend for his last birthday.

Lake Langano is 200 kilometres south of Addis Ababa, Ethiopia, in the Rift Valley. We are lucky to have access to a simple cottage, to which we happily retreat from some of the realities of Ethiopia. The country has yet to recover from the devastating famines of the '80s. Who of my age doesn't remember Bob Geldof's Live Aid fundraising concert for famine relief? And now mothers lament as their sons are sent off to civil war in Tigray, Eritrea, and elsewhere. When will it all end, they must think to themselves.

Langano is a beautiful, dark brown lake enriched with various minerals, including sulphur. It's the only lake in Ethiopia free of bilharzia, the world's second-most-devastating parasitic disease after malaria. A small diesel generator, which coughs politely from time to time, provides all the power we need. Long, grey sandy beaches ring a few small, drab, low-key Soviet-style resorts with a few left from the Emperor Haile Selassie era. The brutal Communist Derg has been in power since 1974 so domestic and international tourists are scarce. Monkeys, baboons, and hippos are all said come to the water's edge to drink and wash but all we have seen are lazy cows led down by small boys waving long sticks from the surrounding farms. Maybe the next time.

Anna and I sip our espressos while sitting on the lawn chairs at the front of the cottage under the African tulip trees. Their soft wood is a favourite for hole-boring nesting birds. I finish my toast and raspberry jam and open an *International Herald Tribune*, the bible of expatriate news junkies in this pre-smartphone and internet world. General Noriega has surrendered in Panama while Marshal Tito's iron forty-five-year rule in Yugoslavia has finally come to an end. Nelson Mandela has been freed after twenty-seven years of imprisonment in South Africa. Maybe Canada's sanctions helped overall. But all of this is, somehow, so far away. Let's enjoy the peace of our surroundings in in this private oasis, I think to myself as I brush crumbs from my lap.

Anna, who is on leave from Parks Canada, where she restores art, flicks her yellow HB pencil every few minutes, then taps on her foolscap pad as she works on the weekly crossword. She wears the beige floppy straw hat she picked up during our brief stopover in Istanbul. Kevin is now building a fort with turrets and gangways, using water he brings in the red pail from the little kitchen. It's amazing how inventive kids can be when given the chance.

We hear the distant musical tinkling of cowbells, almost lost on the soft breeze. A mother calls to her children in Oromo, we presume, a local language neither of us understands. I am embarrassed that I don't even speak Amharic, the *lingua franca* among an astounding seventy-seven spoken in the country. What a rich culture. We have no fixed plan for the day. I will likely continue reading my Graham Greene novel, a pleasant diversion from the outside world, although none is needed here. It's getting warmer as the sun turns brighter overhead. The cool water beckons but we drink another espresso instead. There is no better place to do so, as Ethiopia is the home of coffee, although much of the good product is exported to earn valuable American dollars. Kevin would like to go out fishing in the small black Zodiac raft we picked up in Gatineau before leaving Canada. It takes only a few minutes to inflate with the foot pump. It doesn't matter if we're skunked. In fact, it will be more relaxing if we don't catch anything, as gutting a fish can be messy work. We are at peace.

Figure 5
I lived in Addis Ababa from 1989 to1990 and had access to a wonderful cottage on Lake Langano.

COMPROMISE IN CAMBODIA

As readers will recall, I interviewed thousands of desperate Cambodian refugees straddled along the Thai-Cambodian border for immigration to Canada from 1983-85. Their flight from Cambodia had begun largely after the overthrow of the brutal Khmer Rouge (KR) regime in late 1978. Unfortunately, the installation of the Vietnamese-backed Heng Samrin regime in 1979 did not mean the end of armed conflict. Compounding this state of affairs was the fact that most Western nations (including Canada) chose to recognize the Coalition Government of Democratic Kampuchea (CGDK), which included (incredibly) the Khmer Rouge and two non-Communist factions. The intent of this unprincipled Cold War approach was to deny legitimacy to the Heng Samrin regime as it was indirectly supported by the Soviets. This meant that virtually no international recovery assistance or development aid was made available to Cambodia in the decade following the overthrow of the KR regime. The average Cambodian bore the direct consequences of this calamitous situation, including the absence of any physical, economic, or food security.

In an effort to extricate Cambodia from these seemingly intractable and unfortunate conditions, various international and domestic parties met frequently during the late '80s and early '90s. They eventually signed the *Paris Agreements on a Comprehensive Political Settlement of the Cambodia Conflict,* in 1991. These accords initially facilitated the deployment of the United Nations Advance Mission in Cambodia (UNAMIC), whose ambitious function was to disarm the various factions and create a neutral environment conducive to the eventual conduct of elections. The United Nations Traditional Authority in Cambodia (UNTAC) then came into being, the broader aims of which were to fully restore peace in Cambodia, hold free and fair elections to lead to a new constitution, and "kick-start" the rehabilitation of the country.

Canada was among those countries offering to help in Cambodia. I was keen to participate, given my previous experience with refugees in the region. Although I did have a difficult time believing that the political and military culture of Cambodia could be changed in only a few years and with one election, it was incumbent upon me to at least help try and make this happen in the longer term.

So, in May of 1993, I arranged to be seconded as an international polling station officer (IPSO) with UNTAC. This was just prior to my three-year assignment to the Canadian Consulate General in Minneapolis, so my life was quite hectic over those intervening two months as I prepared for both. I flew from Ottawa to Bangkok, Thailand, and then travelled by bus to the resort town of Jomtien on the Gulf of Siam for three days of intensive training and orientation. I assume that we were sent to the much less known and smaller Jomtien so that participants would not be distracted by the many attractions of nearby Pattaya. It was known for its hedonistic bars, brothels, and beaches. Similarly, it would also have been important to convince the international media and other observers that UNTAC was serious enough in its work not to meet in Pattaya.

Our program included sessions on the background on the mission, Cambodia from 1975 onward, the parties contesting the election, the responsibilities and powers of IPSOs, how to avoid the ubiquitous landmines planted by all sides over the years, and the election process—the focus of our efforts. There was less information on Cambodian cultural sensitivities, however. That would have been useful to ensure we were better able to carry out our duties given that IPSOs were being recruited from around the world and many walks of life. We were also provided with various inoculations and malaria pills, as all of us would be functioning in areas where malaria was known to exist, while other diseases were common and adequate medical care was less available.

The security situation at the time of my arrival was far from peaceful. Although the KR had originally signed the Paris Agreements, they, alone among the various guerilla factions, had refused to disarm and withdrew from the Agreements altogether in 1992 to protest the continuing Vietnamese presence in the country. Various UNTAC civilian and military personnel had been killed or injured in KR attacks over the course of UNTAC's eighteen months of operations prior to our arrival. Deadly incursions against Vietnamese settlers had also occurred. Indeed, the situation was such that voter registration had to be delayed in some regions and the election had to be suspended entirely in others because of security concerns.

From Jomtien we were flown to the Phnom Penh airport in large Soviet military planes. By this time, the Soviet Union had collapsed and Russia was now part of the international effort in Cambodia, including leasing these essential planes to the UN. Very few normal civilian safety precautions were taken on this fight. We had to crouch or sit as best we could on the bare floor in the enormous shell of the plane with our hand luggage scattered around. There were no noise-cancelling headphones to deafen the considerable engine noise. Upon arrival, we were immediately dispatched by Russian military helicopters to various provincial capitals as UNTAC did not want a large group of IPSOs congregating in Phnom Penh. We would have potentially been easy targets for the KR.

I was headed for the small provincial capital of Prey Veng in the province with the same name. Although Prey Veng means "long forest" in Khmer, the main Cambodian language, greedy and wholesale deforestation, which began under the Khmer Rouge, had sadly left little natural vegetation behind. To the east of Phnom Penh, it is Cambodia's third most populous and a primarily rural province. It was one of the worst affected by terrible famine and mass killings under the KR, with thousands buried in mass graves. With the advance of the invading Vietnamese army in January 1979, Prey Veng was one of the first provinces to be liberated from the KR.

To our astonishment, several hundred cheering young children met us at the Prey Veng airport. This was a little disconcerting because we did not feel worthy of such a grand reception. In addition, this could have presented an opportunity for the KR to undertake an attack on or kidnap the children or ourselves. I was billeted for one night in an older western-style house with a personable Western European soldier seconded to UNTAC's military component. The following day, our district teams met with local UNTAC civilian and military officials for further regional briefings, where security was the paramount concern. We then left Prey Veng in a quasi-military procession for our small village in Kamchay Mear district whence we would undertake our electoral duties. I say "quasi" as we travelled by small Japanese pickup trucks with one soldier equipped with a small mounted gun in the back as well as unarmed civilian police (CIVPOL). We did not think that either was particularly well-armed in the event of a KR attack.

Our team of ten IPSOs arrived in mid-afternoon at the little and remote Kamchay Mear UNTAC compound, comprised of various permanent and temporary structures including large incongruous Australian metal trailers and water tanks. The compound was surrounded by five-foot-high barbed wire fences through which curious neighbourhood kids would peer and call to us. Our UNTAC military detachment was comprised of South Asians—Indians, Nepalese, Pakistanis, Bangladeshis, and Sri Lankans. The historical antipathy among the various nations of the Indian subcontinent is well known but I was not aware of any impact it had upon our operations, which is not to say it did not occur.

Our accommodation was far from luxurious. We were housed in simple tents with "porch roofs" so that we did not have to stay inside the entire time while at the compound. For meals we were each provided with dry US army rations to be mixed with boiling water, which we all found to be both tasteless and tedious, hardly a winning culinary combination. Our kitchen was in one of the metal Australian trailers. These were stifling hot when we were preparing our meals due to both the humidity and heat generated by the stove. Some of the IPSOs were unhappy when one of the Cambodian team members used a wok to cook up various flying insects that he'd managed to catch a few minutes earlier. When cooked, these would emit rather noxious smells, but were probably tastier and more nutritious than our fare.

Bathing water was trucked in everyday but there was not always enough left for showers upon our return from our polling stations. This was more than a little exasperating given the 37-degree Celsius temperatures and obvious lack of air conditioning in our tents. Even after a shower we would be sweating profusely. At night we often heard loud rumblings and were never sure whether they were thunderstorms or KR gunfire. There was no incentive to walk around in the early morning or late evening as we had been well warned of landmines on the edge of the village. If is not clear by now, I have to say that my time in the compound was my least favourite during that assignment.

After months of preparation, UNTAC was uncertain as to how the electoral process would go. Would Cambodians come out for the first fair and democratic vote since before the Khmer Rouge? Or did their horrific experiences under the KR scar them permanently? Would there be serious security breaches by the KR? As it turned out, UNTAC had done its job, at least in theory. Ninety-six percent of the eligible national populace had registered to vote and 90 percent of those cast ballots (approximately 4.2 million people). And there were no major security incidents.

Every morning during the election period, we departed in a small convoy, with each IPSO peeling off as they reached their respective polling station. Mine was located underneath a recently constructed Buddhist pagoda in a tiny rural hamlet. I worked with a team of about twenty-five young adult Cambodians, both male and female, eager to make a change in their country. They were also happy to earn a not insignificant income in a country with massive unemployment, as well as to practise their English. This opportunity represented a marked change from the KR regime, which had forbidden the training in or speaking of such "decadent and corrupt" Western languages, possibly punishable with the most severe penalty.

Members of our voting team undertook various tasks, including checking voter registration, instructing voters on how to carry out their new democratic responsibility, and interpreting for me. As most of the voters were illiterate, it was important that they recognize the symbol of the party they wished to vote for and know where to mark their "X." We were delighted to welcome the voters as they trickled into our tiny polling station. As much as they were curious to be exercising their democratic rights for the first time since the KR regime, seeing an actual Caucasian was also a new experience for most. The UNTAC soldiers assigned to our district made only sporadic and inadequate visits. Our safety was otherwise in the hands of a friendly but ill-equipped Cambodian CIVPOL whose equipment consisted of a helmet and metal detector but no weapons whatsoever.

After the voting was completed, IPSOs returned to Prey Veng to count ballots. We worked in a noisy and swelter-ing public hall, rotating shifts around the clock to ensure an early outcome and, thus, instill confidence in the results. We were not always certain who was in the hall with us but local officials tried to reassure us that those present were either scrutineers or other observers authorized to be present. On one occasion, we heard gunfire outside the building but did not know of the exact circumstances. Following the tally process, the results were sent to UN election officials in Phnom Penh for overall tabulation. We then returned to the capital's airport and flew onward to Jomtien, where we were bused to Bangkok for immediate onward departure to our home countries. Sadly, there was no opportunity to provide our views in Jomtien or Bangkok on the voting process, although we were encouraged to submit a short, written report to Elections Canada upon our return. I doubt that many did.

Of the twenty parties that contested the election, FUNCINPEC captured 45 percent of the vote, while the KR's Cambodia's People Party, led by Prime Minister Hun Sen, garnered only 38 percent. This was a disappointment to the latter, although not entirely surprising. Hun Sen had considerable "baggage," as he had been an active KR member in the early '70s and was subsequently appointed foreign minister by the Vietnamese-backed Heng Samrin government. As Hun Sen refused to cede control despite the result, a coalition government led by himself and Prince Ranariddh (loyal to his father, Prince Sihanouk) was formed, a compromise approved by the latter. The relationship between Hun Sen and Prince Ranariddh was rocky and remains strained to this day.

What were my immediate observations of the voting process? I certainly witnessed some unfortunate behaviour by the South Asian military contingent in Kamchay Mear, including the inadvertent breaking of ballot box seals. As far as I could tell, however, there was no intimidation of voters at my polling station by either the KR or other political or military individuals. There were several IPSOs in my contingent from countries that had never held democratic elections themselves, such as South Africa—ironic given the nature of our work. This was because UNTAC had been forced to second reluctant UN officials from around the world to act as IPSOs due to the lack of "volunteers" (who received, by the way, excellent *per diems* intended to compensate for the challenging circumstances).

What did I make of UNTAC's overall role in Cambodia? From a positive perspective, its comprehensive mandate marked the first occasion in which the UN had taken over the entire administration of an independent state and organized and run an election (as opposed to simply monitoring or supervising the process, which I did years later in Ukraine). It was also responsible for promoting and safeguarding human rights at the national level. Secondly, from a logistics perspective, UNTAC successfully managed a huge operation within the allocated timeframe and kept to its US$1.6-billion budget. This needs to be put in the context of a staggering complement of 15,000 military, 3,400 CIVPOLs, and 2,000 IPSOs from over 100 countries as well as 50,000 Cambodian nationals who served as electoral staff. Thirdly, it should be noted that various blocs and individual countries became involved in such a multilateral peacekeeping and civilian operation for the first time, including the former Soviet Union, Japan, China, and neighbouring countries. In the case of Japan, it meant amending their constitution to do so.

In terms of meeting its three objectives, my assessment is more qualified. While UNTAC failed to demobilize the KR military forces, it did manage to disarm the other factions. Fortunately, KR activity, focussed primarily in the remote western provinces, began to dissipate after the election. It evaporated entirely by the late '90s with the death of Pol Pot and the defection or arrest of other leaders. Secondly, while UNTAC was able to undertake the election of 1993 and even declared it a success, few analysts agree wholeheartedly with that assertion, given the very qualified electoral compromise. Finally, it would be difficult to say that UNTAC succeeded in kickstarting the rehabilitation of the country in any meaningful way as we have seen over the last three decades; nor have human rights been promoted and safeguarded.

I was fortunate and glad to have participated in UNTAC's activities. It became clear to me after my return to Canada, however, and over the following years, that UNTAC failed to meet its objectives in many regards. It is probably also true, however, that expectations for its work were overly ambitious. From a career and lifestyle perspective, I began to have second thoughts as to whether I wanted to engage in my chosen career of diplomacy going forward, if this was what it might entail. The world was becoming a more complicated and dangerous place than that which I knew during my first travels to France as an adolescent and when first joining the Foreign Service in 1982. Indeed, I did leave Global Affairs Canada after my subsequent assignment in Minneapolis, to undertake a second master's, at the University of British Columbia. There, I focussed on a very minute and urban Vancouver neighbourhood, far from the world of international diplomacy, but itself the focus of enormous civil conflict and inequity. Although I did return to Ottawa after completion of my degree, I did not choose work that would have required me to live abroad again.

THERE BUT THE GRACE

I have had the great fortune to travel to many countries during my life. In some cases, I have avoided major events or disasters by only a hair's breadth. In 1984 I was travelling near New Delhi, India's capital, when I heard that Prime Minister Indira Gandhi had been assassinated by one of her Sikh bodyguards. Thousands were killed in retaliation during the aftermath although many analysts have predicted that the situation could have been much worse. Indeed, one to two million people were killed during the 1947 partition of British India and millions more displaced due to religious strife. I counted myself lucky to have avoided such a situation thirty seven years later. On another occasion, I left Sri Lanka only three days before the cataclysmic Indian Ocean tsunami.

By way of background, on December 26, 2004, one of the deadliest earthquakes ever began off the Indonesian island of Sumatra, causing a major tsunami that travelled at breakneck speed to twenty-eight countries, killing 228,000 people. Registering a magnitude of 9.1 on the Richter scale, the tsunami produced total global damage that was estimated at US$10 billion. While the worst effects were felt in Indonesia, Sri Lanka was not unscathed. There, 35,000 were killed or disappeared, 21,000 injured, and 516,000 displaced, primarily in the coastal areas of this small nation island southeast of India. The majority of those killed made their living off the sea but, given the speed of the tsunami and the fact they could not swim (a tragic irony), they were unable to escape.

One of the most disturbing events of that day was the death of more than 1,700 people in history's largest single rail disaster. December 26, 2004, began as a busy travel day due to a Buddhist full moon holiday and the Christmas weekend. The Matara Express (pulled, coincidentally, by the General Motors Diesel of Canada locomotive *Manitoba*) departed the Sri Lankan capital of Colombo at 6:50 a.m. on its regular run to Galle, a beautiful, fortified port city to the south. Although Sri Lanka's seismic monitoring station had registered the Sumatran earthquake within minutes of its occurrence, authorities did not believe the tsunami would reach Sri Lanka. Once this grim possibility became a reality, officials immediately halted eight other trains along the coastal line. Sadly, they were unable to reach the Matara Express, as employees were preoccupied with their normal tasks.

The Blue Lotus, the national flower of Sri Lanka, is a symbol of virtue, discipline, and purity.

As the train travelled south, huge ocean waves were thrown up near the town of Telwatta. The train was engulfed and the alarm was sounded. Many villagers rushed toward the train, mistakenly thinking it would offer safe harbour. In only a few minutes, however, the train was picked up and hurled against trees and houses lining the track, quite astonishing when one considers that the locomotive alone weighed at least 260,000 pounds. The eight carriages were so full of panicked passengers trying to flee that the doors could not be opened. As a result, the train quickly filled with water, drowning almost everyone inside as the ocean washed over the wreck several more times. The *Manitoba* ended up in a swamp 100 metres away. Unfortunately, Sri Lankan authorities did not locate the train until 4:00 p.m. that day, at least eight hours later. Even after this, local authorities, emergency services, and the military were naturally overwhelmed by the massive devastation. Local villages were entirely destroyed and the loss of life was considerable.

I was working with the Canadian International Development Agency (CIDA, now part of Global Affairs Canada) when the 2004 Indian Ocean earthquake and tsunami occurred. My responsibilities included the provision of humanitarian assistance in response to civil wars and natural disasters in Asia. I was also tasked with CIDA's relationship with the International Red Cross Movement, which was to play an important role in the tsunami's aftermath. As fortune would have it, I had travelled to Sri Lanka in December of 2004 to meet with various national and international Red Cross officials as well as visit a CIDA-funded project in the northern separatist region, where a brutal civil war had raged for twenty-six years. At the end of the work portion of this trip, I took advantage of the opportunity to do some sightseeing. My itinerary included well known sites such as Anuradhapura (with its well-preserved ruins of an ancient kingdom), Kandy (a former royal capital and sacred Buddhist site), Galle (a fort city on the west coast), and Mirissa (an attractive beach locale on the south coast, where I spent a blissful four nights swimming, walking the beach with the friendly dogs, reading novels, and eating tasty curries).

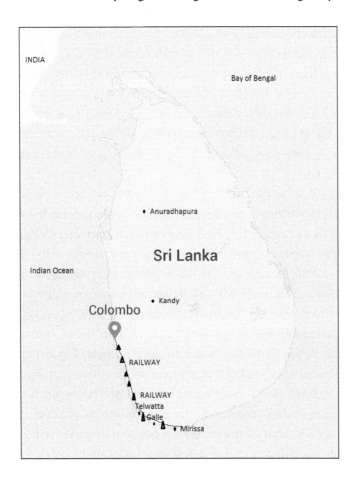

Figure 6
The locations I visited during my December 2004 trip to Sri Lanka.

After packing my bathing suit and snorkel on December 22 at the end of my trip, I boarded an early morning return train to Galle and Colombo to catch my flight back to Canada the next day. In addition to reserved train passengers, as many additional travellers could board as wished to do, including those with government travel permits and railway issued passes. This made for a very sweaty, crowded, noisy, and uncomfortable trip, with frequent stops. While a rapid train today takes just over two hours for the entire trip from Mirissa to Colombo, mine was closer to four due to the age of the locomotive and frequent stops. I recall standing for the entire trip, propping my luggage up against my legs as all the available seats had been taken while others had been removed to provide more standing room. In addition, the average December temperature along the coast is 30 degrees Celsius and, given the somewhat delipidated state of the coaches, there was no air conditioning. So, without access to food or water, I arrived in Colombia exhausted, hungry, and nerve wrecked. The tsunami (the gruesome images of which were constantly replayed in the media) occurred only four days after I had taken the train ride. In the immediate aftermath of the tsunami, I thought of the train being bandied about mercilessly with the attendant loss of life. I might have been on board had my schedule been only a few days different. Indeed, I had considered spending the holiday season in Sri Lanka so might easily have done so.

As soon as I got back to Canada, I travelled to Toronto to spend a few days' holiday with my brother and sister-in-law. As news of the extraordinary tsunami and its catastrophic consequences became known, I headed back to Ottawa early. I was soon called in to assist in Canada's humanitarian response. Colleagues were brought on board in Gatineau (part of the National Capital Region) from different programs to assist while others were deployed to the affected areas in Asia to assess needs and monitor the response. In typical government fashion, multiple committees and task forces were struck at all levels. My colleagues and I worked many long hours in the evenings and weekends over the coming months facilitating Canada's unprecedented US$750 million in grants and contributions. This amount compared very favourably to the overall US$13.5 billion donor response to various organizations, including United Nations agencies, the Red Cross and non-governmental organizations (NGOs) such as Oxfam, Care, and World Vision. We were extremely lucky that we were able approve such humanitarian funding in as little as forty-eight hours compared to development projects, which can often take years to develop and approve.

Whether the international community's response to the tsunami was as effective as it could have been could be debated for a long time. I am not sure that all the necessary data and evidence will ever be available to make that judgement. On the negative side, post-disaster needs assessments relating to water, food, shelter, and primary care were rarely coordinated or shared among humanitarian actors, which resulted in some needs not being met in a timely fashion and duplication of services in other cases. There was also pressure to spend money quickly and visibly by bringing equipment and supplies from outside the region, thus not fully maximizing local economies and capacities where available, particularly during the transition from relief to recovery. As usual, there were problems with unqualified actors and inappropriate donations such as expired medications being made available. Compounding these realities in Indonesia and Sri Lanka were ongoing internal military conflicts, lack of capacity, corruption, and bureaucracy.

But there is no question that without the efforts of the domestic and international community, the situation would have been much worse. In Sri Lanka, for example, 80 percent of damaged fish markets, boats, and equipment were fully restored in short order, thus allowing much of the local population to recommence their lives as best they could.

In retrospect, I obviously consider myself blessed to have left Sri Lanka four days before this catastrophe and proud to have contributed in my small way to Canada's response. How I avoided the tragedy is something I have asked myself on a few occasions. Was it karma, luck, or divine intervention? This is something else I will never know.

A FEW THOUGHTS ON
THE HERMIT KINGDOM

My desire to visit the Democratic People's Republic of Korea (DPRK) or North Korea, as it is commonly known, went back several years. I had always had a peculiar fascination for Communist regimes. I had managed to visit Cuba in 1977, before it more fully opened up to Western tourism and became fashionable. I spent a fascinating two weeks in Yugoslavia in 1978, when it was still a unified (not necessarily happily) socialist country under Marshall Tito. I also travelled to Vietnam and Laos for work purposes between 1983 and 1985, prior to Western tourists being allowed. None of these countries made travel easy and perhaps that was one of the attractions.

While at the Canadian International Development Agency toward the end of my professional career, I had a "watching brief" for the DPRK, which meant little more than monitoring the limited media reports and appeals for humanitarian assistance. Although I tried to follow events there, that was difficult due to the dearth of information from any reliable source. What was clear was that the DPRK was experiencing major difficulties brought on by the end of the Soviet economic system, from which North Korea had benefitted greatly since before its foundation in 1945. It was also suffering from recurring devastating famines due to severe weather as well as government mismanagement.

I had hoped to arrange a visit to the capital, Pyongyang, to assess the situation I have described and determine whether and how Canada might provide humanitarian assistance in response to the crisis. Unfortunately, my superiors did not place a high priority on this matter, either in terms of the actual needs on the ground or the potential political ramifications of such a visit. Such a trip might have been taken by some as a change in Canadian foreign policy, which was not in the cards at that time or even now.

So, if I were going to get to North Korea (sometimes also referred to as the Hermit Kingdom due to its isolationist policies), it would be of my own accord. When I finally retired in 2014 after thirty years with the government of Canada, I decided to give myself a lavish present of a ten-week trip to East Asia. My stops would include Mongolia, Bhutan, Tibet (part of China contrary to the wishes of its ethnic Tibetan inhabitants), and North Korea, as well as India, Nepal, and China, three countries I had already had to the pleasure of visiting years earlier. This trip took many months to plan, due partly to the fact that I had to determine what travel was even possible in a finite amount of time given the vast distances, limited transportation networks, and costs. I also needed to get visas for all the countries I was to visit. Mongolia, Tibet, Bhutan, and North Korea necessitated that I go as part of a group or solo package tour. It was important that I get these tours back-to-back so as not to waste too much time cooling my heels between each country.

During my ten-day excursion to the Hermit Kingdom, I managed to visit the capital of Pyongyang and the high-security and sensitive Demilitarized Zone (DMZ) along the border with South Korea, a popular tourist destination by North Korean standards. If truth be told, however, the trip from Seoul, the capital of South Korea, to the DMZ is much more revealing as it is easier to see what is happening along the North Korean border in terms of the military presence and exercises. Another stop was at the Nampo West Sea Barrage, a massive feat of civil engineering intended to control tides and permit port operations without beaching ships, prevent large scale flooding, protect farmland, and revitalize the region's agriculture. Whether the project has succeeded in some or all its objectives is debateable. There has also probably been some environmental damage due to the project although it would be difficult to get any objective quantitative data on this. The fourth major destination was Mount Paektu on the Chinese border to the north, which I shall discuss shortly.

Finally, I should mention the Friendship Exhibitions near Mount Myohyang, several hours northeast of Pyongyang. This was a sight the likes of which I had not seen before or at least not on that scale. Here, two massive traditional Korean-style buildings house the world's gifts to the two senior Kims, the country's dynastic leaders, ranging from Kalashnikov-shaped vodka bottles to one of Mao's railway carriages. From my experience, commemorating rail travel in former Communist countries is almost *de rigeur*. I also visited the coach of the former Soviet leader Josef Stalin in his native Georgia a few years later. Those having presented gifts to the Kims include the American evangelist Billy Graham (quite an anomaly for a country diametrically opposed to Christianity) and sympathetic workers' groups from Canada and elsewhere. Solemn guards are equipped with silver-plated machine guns so it's best be on good behaviour.

Preparations before stepping inside the buildings are elaborate. Visitors are provided with white gloves in case they care to open the massive four-tonne bronze-coloured doors. Hats must be taken off and cameras checked. I am not sure what is particularly sensitive about these gifts that can't be captured on film, however. Visitors must also don baggy socks to cover their shoes before they dutifully shuffle by a mind-boggling 71,000 gifts, meticulously categorized by continent and chronology in one hundred windowless rooms. This must have been a daunting and exhausting task for the curators and is equally intimidating for the visitor.

If readers are interested in travelling to North Korea and wish to know more about specific other cities and sights, sample tours can be found on the websites of the half dozen Western operators authorized by the DPRK government under non-COVID circumstances. What I will do now is provide some observations based on my trip and the monitoring of traditional media in the years before and after.

Firstly, North Korea is not easy to get to, a I have already mentioned; neither is travel around the cities or attractive countryside with its many mountains, coasts, and pristine rivers easy. The regime granted as few as 8,000 visas for Western tourists per year throughout for the entire country in those pre-pandemic days. Now, of course, the borders are entirely sealed. Under normal circumstances, tourists must visit on guided and strictly regulated tours, as was the case with my trip. Access to many parts of the country is prohibited and foreigners' movements in areas where they are permitted are controlled and closely monitored. They tend to see only the best conditions and not the deprivation, malnutrition, and shortages that consistently plague the DPRK.

Many travellers spend considerable time in Pyongyang, an artificial showcase of the "best" the country has to offer. The capital is noteworthy for its deliberately designed street grid and increasing number of skyscrapers, which are increasingly lit at night these days. Past visitors were struck by the nighttime darkness of the city, a not entirely unpleasant experience compared to the frenetic pace of other Asian capitals. Sadly, restaurant food at the prescribed locales is often hit and miss due to food availability and the fact that several tour buses usually arrive at one time.

This means that food must be made in large quantities some time in advance so suffers from a certain buffet or cafeteria effect.

Many conveniences westerners took for granted in those days such as internet cafes and automatic tellers simply did not exist. Toilet facilities outside Pyongyang can be truly atrocious, particularly at remote significant tourist destinations outside the major cities.

Another conspicuous aspect of the DPRK is the historical distrust of foreigners, a sentiment actually fostered by the DPRK government. Their experiences, after all, with the Chinese, Japanese, and American occupations and wars were not positive. During a visit to a children's day care, we were informally treated to songs cheerfully describing military attacks upon Americans, hardly likely to win the confidence of most Western tourists.

A second feature of the DPRK is the prevalent "Kim cult," evident to Western tourists immediately upon landing at the Pyongyang airport and during the drive to the hotel. Everywhere are images of the Hermit Kingdom's only and successive leaders since the Korean armistice of 1953: The Great Leader Kim Il-Sung, his son the Dear Leader Kim Jong-Il, and his son and current Brilliant Leader, Kim Jong-Un. Statues of and political treatises by the Great and Dear Leaders dominate the vast Kim Il-Sung Square in Pyongyang and are oddly and strategically etched in mountainsides throughout the country. North Koreans and foreigners alike are required to pay respect to such shrines by giving a solitary nod in front of the site but also by presenting flowers on occasion. Although this can be a little unnerving for Westerners, failure to do so is usually not an option. The Kims also grace the covers of most official travel publications. Even accidentally covering an image of Jong-Il on a magazine cover in one's hotel room was an offence I took pains to avoid should the cleaning staff enter my room during my absence. Finally, the Kims' wisdom and the guiding DPRK philosophy of *Juche*, which affirms that human beings are the masters and arbiters of everything, are infused in every North Korean's class, from day care to university.

The regime has total control over both the state apparatus and individual lives of its citizens. The Governing Korean Workers' Party (which the Dear Leader used to ascend to power) rarely meets and automatically approves all of the Kims' decisions. Potentially oppositional threats to the regime or actions considered inappropriate by the Kims at even the most senior levels are not tolerated and may result in prison camp, disappearance, or worse, as demonstrated by the execution of Jong-Un's uncle, Jang Song Thaek, soon after the young Kim's assumption of power. Absolute control over individuals extends to the information sphere, as all but a few privileged members of the regime have no access to any objective sources of news. Indeed, North Korea ranks last among 180 countries in the World Press Freedom Index. If the tour guides' speaking routine was to be believed, North Korean citizens honestly contend that their system is far more successful in terms of economic and social development than South Korea, which overtook them by all objective analyses in the 1970s.

The myths propagated by the Kims to enhance their stature among North Korean citizens as part of their Stalinist personality are legendary. A case in point is the assertion that Dear Leader Kim Jong-Il was born in a log cabin on the slopes of Mount Paektu, a site that plays important mythological and cultural roles in the societies and civil religions of both Koreas. This claim would seem to be in contradiction with Russian records indicating that Jong-Il was born in the Siberian village of Vyatskoye. The distance between these two places is as much as 2,700 kilometres, by my rough calculation. And when I saw the "original" cabin at Mount Paektu, it looked to have been assembled from a kit ordered from an outdated Sears catalogue. What was even more striking was that the building did not appear to have a chimney, which would have been essential for heat in the cold mountain winters and for cooking year round.

Another interesting affirmation was that the Dear Leader shot thirty-eight under par during his first ever round of golf, including eleven holes in one. This remarkable feat would have been the envy even of Jack Nicklaus or Tiger Woods, the two greatest names in the history of men's golf. An equally bizarre proclamation was that Kim Jong-Un never needed to urinate or defecate, presumably because he is considered a deity rather than a mere mortal. This reference was later removed from the government website, likely due to the incredulous reaction it provoked in the Western media.

A final observation regarding the regime's strict control relates to the fact those very few foreign guidebooks that have been written over the years on the Hermit Kingdom can be brought into the country. I suspect this is due both to a traditional suspicion of anything foreign and because any negative depiction of life in North Korea or the regime would not be tolerated. It would obviously be hard to write an entirely complementary volume given some of the things I have mentioned already. We were also advised by our western tour operators that the authors of the Bradt third edition guide (which I succeeded in taking into the DPRK and consulted in drafting this life story) committed the sin of accidentally and minutely cropping part of the Great Leader's arm in its cover photo, rendering the book inadmissible at North Korean customs.

Have I put you off yet? Would I recommend visiting the cloistered Hermit Kingdom? In answering these questions, I am reminded of an *Economist* article I read thirty-two years ago, which described travelling in the then equally isolated and extreme Albania as "a thinking person's holiday" rather than an enjoyable experience. So, too, is the case with the DPRK. If your primary emphases in travel are on comfort, relaxation, familiarity, and amusement, then the Hermit Kingdom is not for you. I have to admit that I was a little tired by the end of my ten days given the conditions and packed schedule. But if you are prepared to rough it and to adapt to challenges and circumstances as they arise, then you should consider going. Curious travellers will be rewarded by many attractive natural sights. I was also fascinated by how such a country could even exist in the twenty-first century. I am particularly glad to have visited when I did as the DPRK may undergo a major shift depending on a possible succession to Jong-Un, who is sometimes rumoured to be unwell despite his young age.

As a result of my brief excursion, I am certainly better able to assess Western news stories on the Hermit Kingdom. But at what price? Much of the money I paid for my tour found its way into the coffers of the Kim family and government of North Korea, thus providing financial support to a financially bankrupt and repressive regime. This makes me a little ambivalent but I leave it to the reader and potential traveller to decide whether they would be comfortable with that themselves.

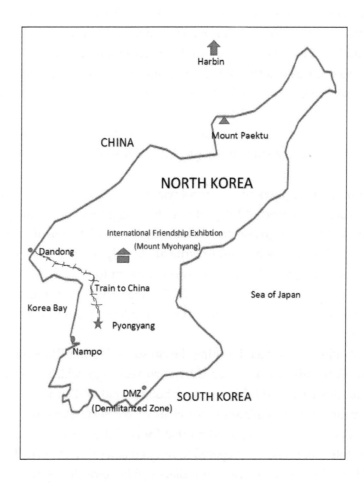

Figure 7

My stops on a fascinating trip to North Korea.

AFTERWORD

I chose to title this book *On the Border* because more than half of the life stories take place in another country, thus necessitating the crossing of a border of some sort, whether literal or figurative, by myself as author or by you as reader. The cover photograph is of a hamlet close to the French and Andorran border not far from Spain, an area which I love and in which I have spent some time. *On the Border* is also the title of one of the life stories that describes my work interviewing Cambodian refugees wishing to immigrate to Canada. These refugees had experienced an appalling descent into hell during the Khmer Rouge regime, as readers are aware. After the regime's downfall, those in the refugee camp were straddled on the literal and figurative border between a new life in Canada and a return to an uncertain future in Cambodia. A second life story pertains to my 1993 experiences as an international polling station officer in Cambodia itself, when the country itself was on a border of another sort. Cambodia was traversing a frontier between a potentially peaceful and prosperous future and a return to darkness. The intent of my work as an international polling station officer during the election was to help Cambodians traverse this boundary, which they have done only tentatively, unfortunately.

I am particularly appreciative of Anouk'Chet Suong for providing the rich illustrations accompanying each life story. Thanks to Marlyne for expertly photographing these illustrations and to Étienne for ensuring the correct map formats. I am grateful to my sister and brothers (Barbara, David, and Peter) for helping me to reflect on certain events and dimensions related to my family more accurately. I am also indebted to various friends and former colleagues for reading drafts and providing background and context as needed. These include Deborah Dunton, Kurt Egloff, Jack Gibbons, Flora Liebich and Stephen Randall. And thanks to Dilshad Macklem and Ian Thomas Shaw for explaining more of the publishing business to me.

Credit for the map of the United Kingdom (Figure 2) goes to Vector Stock, while the cover photo is from Adobe Stock. Credit goes to freevectormaps.com for the map of Sri Lanka. The Robert Service verse was taken from the collection *Songs of a Sourdough*. Martha Edmond's *Rockcliffe Park: A History* provided useful context for *Operation Ginger*. David P. Chandler's *A History of Cambodia* and Michael Molloy's *Running on Empty: Canada and the Indochinese Refugees, 1975-80* were helpful in getting some of the facts related to "*On the Border*" and "*Compromise in Cambodia*" straight. Robert Willoughby's *North Korea: The Bradt Travel Guide* was useful in recalling my visit to that country.

I express appreciation to the team at FriesenPress for essential editing and publishing services and marketing advice, which made this book possible.

CPSIA information can be obtained
at www.ICGtesting.com
Printed in the USA
LVHW011247241121
704326LV00004B/366

9 781039 114050